THIS
KIND OF
SILENCE

How Losing My Hearing
Taught Me to Listen

Michele Susan Brown

Copyright 2019 by Michele Susan Brown

First published by Joanne Fedler Media, 2019

www.joannefedler.com (publisher's website)
www.marketingmentor.live (design by Nailia Minnebaeva)

Printed in Australia, UK, and USA.

National Library of Australia Cataloguing-in-Publication data:
ISBN 978-1-925842-09-8 (Paperback)
ISBN 978-1-925842-10-4 (Hardback)
ISBN 978-1-925842-11-1 (Ebook)

For Mom and Dad, Brennan and Trevor, and Gordon

A Letter to My Reader

The quieter you become, the more you hear.
—Ram Dass

Dear Reader,

Writing this book and birthing it to the world is a dream come true. It's been a labor of love for over five years, and most importantly, an agreement I've honored with myself.

This memoir accurately reflects my own experience, and has been based upon memories, journal entries, and conversations with characters involved.

I realize as this book makes its entrance, that I'm sharing a deeply personal story. The essence of who I am, in fact, and that is a little scary. My truth, my vulnerability, my rawness, has spilled out and onto these pages. Personal growth is just that—personal.

I'm sure there will be some discomfort for some in my life that read these pages, but my hope is that the good will outweigh any unintentional pain caused.

I hope you find in this story inspiration, helpfulness, and hope that will give you permission to journey into your own caves of self. I feel as though my heart calls to yours to tell you that you are not alone in times of deep confusion and struggle. Sometimes, the answers can be found by turning your gaze inward rather that outward.

May you take time to listen to the whispers of wisdom within you.

With love,
Michele

CHAPTER 1

2014

I t's one of the first short-sleeved spring evenings of 2014 at our home in Northern California. Teriyaki chicken sizzles on the barbecue while a medley of bird song fills the backyard air, and palm trees dance with the breeze. My husband, Gordon, carries his worn leather briefcase to the kitchen table and tells me he'd like to discuss the possibility of an upcoming trip. As he starts talking, my mind dances back to our most recent adventures: swimming with mother and calf humpback whales in the Dominican Republic, and touring ornate castles and medieval towns in Central Europe. I glance over at the large world map hanging in our living room, noting the red pins, which mark all the places we've been, and the blue ones, marking destinations on our wish list.

When Gordon pours us each a glass of chardonnay and reveals a manila folder with a boyish grin, I'm daydreaming about some of those blue pins: the Maldives, Australia, Galapagos Islands, Thailand.

"Well, it's a," he motions the sound of a drum roll, "trip to Antarctica!"

Surely, he just said Antigua or Anguilla in the Caribbean, right? I can't find the words to answer him right away, so I just let him keep talking.

"It's a November ski trip with a company called Ice Axe Expeditions."

He opens and unfolds a brochure, reading aloud every single detail of the (packed) twelve-day itinerary. I concentrate on the sound of his deep voice. It's one of the things I love most about Gordon. Like a skilled radio or television announcer with perfect inflection and tone, he projects strength and confidence, gently commanding attention. He's been an avid skier his whole life and goes heli-skiing every year in Canada, and as he talks me through the plans for the trip, I hear his raw enthusiasm and feel the wonder through his words. When I ask about skiing without chair lifts, he explains how people train in advance to "skin up" glaciers— attaching a non-sliding fabric to the bottom of skis to essentially climb up a glacier, remove the fabric, and then ski back down.

"You should go! Wow, honey, it sounds right up your alley!" The words flow off my tongue because I genuinely mean them. Climbing a glacier wearing skis sounds like just the thing Gordon would love. But when I look up at him, Gordon's calculating hazel eyes are staring back at me.

"But I...uh...I want you to come with me."

I can tell he sees both my eyebrows raise and stay frozen there.

"This is, well, it's Antarctica, Michele. People I've talked to say it's the trip of a lifetime. Antarctica is a place very few people ever see. I want to experience it with you."

"But...I don't ski...and...I...." My voice cracks. I take a sip of wine.

"You don't have to ski. There will be other people there who don't, either. But you can enjoy activities like visiting penguin rookeries, and I hear the scenery is unbelievable. You'll love taking photos!" Images of penguins and glaciers swim through my mind as he continues. "Look, I really can't imagine not sharing an experience like this with you. I'd like you to go with me."

Gordon says the last three words extra slowly and moves toward me. I feel the nervous knots in my stomach ease when he wraps his arms around me. I've always wanted a team-like togetherness, and this moment is just another reminder that I have it. Right here, in front of me. Even though my breath feels a little shallow in my chest, and a list of unknowns parade through my head, I hear an inner voice of knowingness whisper that I can trust that I'll be safe.

"Umm, okay," I say with a sprinkle of hesitation, slowly nodding my head. "I always said I would go anywhere in the world with you. I just, I honestly never thought it would include Antarctica."

I lay my head against Gordon's broad chest and listen to his throaty, contagious laughter while he wraps me in an enthusiastic squeeze.

Six months later, we're walking up a narrow white metal staircase to board a ship called the *Sea Adventurer*. It's now November in 2014, springtime in Ushuaia, Terra Del Fuego in Argentina—the southernmost city of the world. Our accommodation for the next eleven nights isn't on a grand cruise ship with pools, glass elevators, and spa treatments by Royal Caribbean or Princess. No, this is a retrofitted, antique Russian Icebreaker. I notice the huge thick steel hull that forms into a sharp triangle at the bow and realize this is a serious expedition ship created for turbulent waters and specifically for crossing the infamous Drake Passage.

Over the course of the last six months, I've studied Antarctica and read about the Drake Passage, where the Pacific, Atlantic, and Indian Oceans converge. It's well known as the roughest of all passages and will likely take forty-eight hours to cross. *Forty-eight.* As Gordon and I take our final step across the ship's threshold, hand in hand, and step into a parlor of red velvet chairs bolted to the floor, it hits me that we're heading to the coldest, windiest, emptiest place on Earth. There is no turning back. I take a deep breath while my fingers wander up to feel the Scopolamine patch placed behind my ear. I also have an Ativan in my purse. Just in case.

As the ship pulls away from the harbor, I look through large windows and watch buildings, cars, slopes of green trees, and snow-covered peaks fade from view. Casually dressed adventurers mingle in the dining room. Gordon pulls me into one of the huddles, introduces us, and shares that we have a winter cabin at Squaw Valley. The scene reminds me of pack animals. Looking around, I see mostly men between the ages of thirty-five and fifty-five. They all have the same athletic, lean, natural, and rugged appearance, and exude an air of experienced confidence. Clothing from Patagonia and North Face fills the room. I detect a frenetic energy while listening to comparisons and questions like, "How many vertical feet did you get in last year?" Or, "My goal this season is to ski a hundred and twenty days." As they all nod and laugh, I shift my feet from side to side to mask self-consciousness. I revel in my ability to overhear the locations repeatedly mentioned in other nearby conversations: Tahoe City, Jackson Hole, British Columbia, Park City, Chamonix, Swiss Alps, even Russia. One thing is clear: everyone here radiates comfort with winter. They crave glaciers and snowy mountains to climb up and ski down.

Not a skier, snowboarder, trekker, or mountain-terrain enthusiast, I much prefer places where I can wander around barefoot, clad in a tank top and shorts. Where warm breezes, salty ocean sprays, and loud crashing waves permeate the air. In these settings, I breathe much more freely and expansively than I am now, as I desperately search for something to add to the conversation.

Later that night, I learn that out of one hundred and two guests, I am only one of five non-skiing participants. Knowing that I am the odd one out awakens a familiar discomfort. But I'm jolted out of my self-consciousness when I see multiple fingers point out the windows. I squint my eyes to see what's grabbed everyone's attention. A bright double rainbow emerges from the ocean water and arcs the entire sky. I grab my camera, enticed by this welcoming omen, and run out to the deck to shoot it. My camera clicks rapidly, a comforting sound, as I attempt to capture the vibrant stacks of red, orange, yellow, and green pouring into the white-capped blue below. Gordon joins me with a warm hand on my back. As I pull my head back from the viewfinder and take in the panoramic scene, I feel as though I've been given a kiss of peace and hope. I wish I could freeze this moment in time.

On the second day at sea, land is no longer in sight, and the swell of the waves grows more powerful. An albatross with his white head and dark eyebrow smudge flies with grace overhead, his impressive wingspan on display. The only sounds on the ship as we make our journey into the desolate silence of the open ocean are the lull of the engine and the spray of the ship's wake. Albatrosses and southern giant petrels hover over whitecaps as we head further into the unknown. While the sun shines brightly through a few clouds, the wind cuts sharply through my jacket and long-sleeved shirt.

There must be thirty others sitting with Gordon and me on the

THIS KIND OF SILENCE

stern deck in portable chairs unlocked from cables. Some people read books, Kindles, type on iPads, watch movies with headphones, snooze, or listen to music. Others chat about skiing and sip a beer or glass of white wine. Several repeat travelers comment that they've never seen the seas like this.

"Usually, it's Drake Shake. This is Drake Lake!" says Andrew, a well-known ski guide from Park City, Utah, who's chalked up over twenty mountaineering expeditions.

I smile gratefully and sigh a breath of relief, looking around at the sunshine bouncing off the ship, the calm and serene ocean beyond.

The following day, Gordon and I stand side by side on the ship's deck dressed in five layers of clothing and hats covering our ears. My nose runs and white puffs leave my lips on every exhale. We grip the wooden handrail with our gloved hands as the ship rocks up and down more than side-to-side. The public address system crackles before the captain's distinct Russian accent blares, "We're approaching the South Shetland Islands, still sailing through the Drake Passage with more turbulence than prior hours." It's true. No one is just sitting around today—and I spy all the chairs once again fastened together with thick cables.

While breathing my way through the turbulence, I spot a big blow of ocean spray on the starboard side. Then another. And a third one. "Look, honey—whales!" I exclaim while tugging on Gordon's jacket. Each powerful exhale mixes with the lingering sprays of the last, creating a continuous shower of mist and a song of the slow, laboring sounds of blowholes. A crowd gathers around the railing, many with SLR cameras and GoPros in hand. Someone counts eighteen whales, then another soon raises it to twenty-four

The captain's voice interjects, "These herds of humpback whales are probably feeding on krill swarms just beneath the surface.

I anticipate they're heading north, to South Africa, Australia, New Zealand, or America. I will slow down the ship because there are about fifty of them right now." Long white pectoral fins about sixteen feet long take on a tropical blue reflection just below the surface of the cold waters. We are surrounded.

I link my elbow through Gordon's arm and squeeze. All of us spectators have become a human pod, quiet, present, focused, sharing in the wonder of the powerful sprays and showy flicks of tail flukes as the whales dive below. Silence follows whispered *wows*. No land in sight, no other vessels in view, it's just us standing along the ship rail in complete awe. I close my eyes to listen more intently, focusing on the sounds of these majestic mammals and the silent stillness of our surroundings, reveling in my ability to hear.

For it wasn't always so.

CHAPTER 2

NOVEMBER 1997

I feel a black emptiness inside me. It nags at me for attention. I don't know why it's here or what it wants from me; I just want it to leave. But every time I ignore it, it resurfaces.

Just like an oil slick appears on a pristine beach, various and odd health issues have begun to surface in my life. Chest pain—as if a stranger has snuck up behind me and is stabbing me near the heart. The sharp discomfort radiates through to my back. When this happens, I take some slow deep breaths in hopes of clearing the pain. Sometimes I touch the site, gently pressing into the tissue that houses the hurt, wondering why I can feel a soreness, like a wound of some sort that didn't exist just minutes before. This unknown ache lingers for moments, minutes, hours—it's unpredictable—and visits me at home, work, or when I'm driving. Each time, I wonder whether I am about to have a heart attack. Finally, I see the regular doctor I've had since I was fifteen just to make sure I'm not about to die.

"Your blood pressure is excellent, temperature normal, and you're thirty-two years old with no family history of heart conditions, heart disease, or cancer, Michele. I'm perplexed."

I don't know how to respond. I do feel like an otherwise healthy, fit, vibrant woman. An awkward silence lingers.

"Are things going well in your life? Are you feeling depressed?" He drops his chin and looks over the top of his spectacles at me, revealing his unruly eyebrows.

"No, everything is going fine. Except for this. I have no reason to be depressed," I respond. I'm positive that I don't resemble a depressed individual, and his suggestion annoys me.

"Well, it sounds like what you're experiencing is anxiety," he states matter-of-factly, pronouncing "anxiety" slowly as if to accentuate each syllable.

"What causes that?" I ask, expecting to learn how to un-cause it.

"Could be a number of things, including depression and stress. I'll give you a script for Xanax to take when needed." He scribbles on a note-sized tablet, tears off the page, and hands it to me with a gracious smile.

As I leave his office, I am sure it must be stress. It makes the most sense. The stress of my job as the principal of an elementary school, stress of juggling work and mothering two young boys, stress of a long work commute. Everyone in our thirties age group of professional career couples with young children is striving to find the balance. I'm no exception. And I know I should be happy that I've been married for almost eight years and live in a nice house in a good neighborhood. But as I think about it, I realize that the household work *has* been getting more demanding lately. My husband Al is the type who's eager and willing to fix a rickety fence or build a new brick walkway in the front yard while wearing shorts and a tank top;

but cooking, cleaning, laundry, and diaper changing aren't quite on his list of priorities. He calls these things "women's work." I see that I've been carrying most of the load at home while also working full time and not complaining. Maybe it's just getting to me.

I think back on the conversation Al and I had on this topic last week while in bed before going to sleep,

"I just feel like maybe my job is getting to me. You know, all the stress. I don't know if I like my job," I had said.

His response had been predictable. "No one *likes* their job, Michele. That's why it's called work. It's just something we have to do. Don't overthink it."

During the drive home, I tell myself:

It's just stress. Lots of people have it. I'm not depressed.

My God, I don't have anything to be depressed about.

It's not like I can't handle it or anything.

I have two beautiful little boys, a husband of seven years, a successful career. Right?

I should be happy.

Anxiety…whatever. It will go away. It has to.

After pulling off the freeway, I drive under the towering canopies of grand oak trees along Land Park Drive in Sacramento. A wide street full of quaint, character-rich homes and well-manicured lawns, I see couples walking hand in hand or pushing strollers, and children riding bicycles. By the time I turn right onto Seventh Avenue and our driveway comes into view, I've diagnosed myself with an annoying minor blip in the otherwise great life I am living. I decide to focus more on being positive and to get past this.

But while vice-like chest pains I've attempted to ignore persist, a new physical intruder emerges—this time, more hostile.

CHAPTER 3

EARLY MARCH 1998

I wake up on March 10, 1998, and I can't hear.

Opening my eyes, I feel a pressure in my right ear that wasn't there the day before—a plugged-up-ness. I keep trying to yawn or swallow like I do on an airplane. It feels like I'm descending underwater and I need to acclimatize to the altitude change, but I can't. Nothing helps clear it. I get up and go about my morning, but the longer the sensation lingers, the more annoyed I become while getting ready for work. I'm rushing again, and I don't have time for this irritation while I check off my mental to do's: *pack the diaper bag for Trevor with bottles and formula, remember jars of Gerber, leave the filled-out envelope with check enclosed for Brennan's preschool picture day on the counter, put out the clothes for Brennan to wear, place the empty Alhambra bottled water container on the porch to be picked up and replenished.* Thank goodness Al has been dropping off the boys in the mornings, one less thing to do. I tap at my ear a couple of times. No change, except now there's a weird hum inside my head too.

I settle in my car for the thirty-minute commute from Old Land Park to Roseville, and turn up the volume to listen to one of six favorite CDs in the changer. Madonna, Mariah Carey, Sarah McLachlan, Jewel, Celine Dion, and Elton John have been on constant rotation lately. Which one will guide me to work today? As soon as it comes on, the music sounds weird. Is my stereo working properly? All I can seem to hear is the drumbeat. The other instruments are muted, and the vocals are garbled. In fact, I don't recognize the song. I can't even tell who's singing! I panic and push the forward button to change to the next one. Same thing. I decide to switch to FM radio instead. I hear talking. A male voice, but I can't understand what he's saying. I frown, look at the stereo display, and hit it gently twice, wondering if there is a bad wiring connection or something. More fuzziness fills my car when I turn up the volume. Flustered and annoyed, I punch the off button. Enough.

But then I discover that no noise is also unsettling. A humming coupled with a mild whooshing sound swirl around inside my head. While I know my right ear is filled with an unusual pressure of sorts, I wonder if I can't hear at all because both my ears are affected. There's low constant buzz that I don't recognize. And this time, there isn't a switch to turn it off. When I arrive at Kaseberg Elementary School where I have been a principal for two years, I feel relieved that it is not a staff-meeting morning. I'm not in my usual cheery, upbeat mood. I am irritable, unsettled, and anxious.

I drop my purse on my office desk and walk out to my favorite place at work, the playground, during early morning recess. I watch children play hopscotch and tetherball on the blacktop. But the shoes jumping on the asphalt and fists hitting the swinging ball don't sound like they usually do. I can hardly hear these familiar noises at all. The sunshine feels gentle, but the winds sound too strong.

Grammar school voices and laughter drift away with each gust. I'm relieved when two first grade girls run toward me so I can shift my focus to them.

"Mrs. Marshall! Can we walk around with you?" I hear Amber's high-pitched tone and watch her flash a toothless grin.

"Of course you can!" My own voice sounds like I'm speaking from a tunnel. I offer them a hand on each side of me.

We walk together toward the grass where upper grade boys play soccer. Mr. Hartshorn, one of the third grade teachers on supervision duty, greets us. His eyes are bright as his lips move, but his words are muffled. I think he's asked me a question, but I'm not sure.

"Can you say that again, please?" I step in closer. A kicked black and white soccer ball sails over both our heads, and two boys run after it.

"How are you today?" Mr. Hartshorn says, more slowly this time. I wonder if that's what he really asked a moment ago. The collective noise of hundreds of children running and playing around us is all I can seem to hear.

"I…I'm actually having a rough morning. My ears feel all plugged up." I touch my right ear and open my jaw to see if I can relieve the constant feeling of pressure in my head. Nothing changes.

"It's probably allergies." He speaks louder, but I watch his lips form the words in order to understand. "The wind is blowing all kinds of stuff around."

"Probably," I say with a nod as the bell rings.

The girls hug my legs tight and wave goodbye. I watch them run, eager to line up by their classroom while I walk back across the blacktop through my head fog toward the office.

The remaining hours of this day are drawn out and bleak. I pick up pieces of conversations but I clearly miss more than I should, and I know it when I receive puzzled faces in response to what I say.

I'm trying over and over to clear the pressure in my head by yawning, swallowing, or holding my nose closed and blowing. I borrow Sudafed tablets and ignore the worry bubbling up inside me. I feel as though bricks of annoyance and irritation are being piled on top of my chest. In a rare move, I decide to spend the whole afternoon sitting at my desk doing paperwork, my office door closed.

Eager to go home by the end of the day, I walk through the office door into the parking lot and notice a nearby bulldozer and a construction crew working on the main street. I pause to listen. How can even the noise from a jackhammer be dampened?

Thinking about this for a few minutes takes me back in time to my college days at Chico State University in 1984.

On the way back from class, walking across the residence hall parking lot of South Hall, I hear a roar of power followed by a deep rumble. A royal blue two-door 1972 Pontiac Firebird with oversized tires and a large shiny silver engine pipe on the front hood shakes in a parking space ahead. The license plate reads BLUMAGC, and the driver, while not moving the car forward, accelerates several times and creates a rhythm of noise. Two large shiny mufflers spew bursts of smoke with each elongated purr. As I get closer, I watch the driver roll down his window. Al smiles without showing his teeth. He's got shoulder-length dark hair that's obviously just been blow-dried, styled, moussed, maybe even hair sprayed. He smells of Polo cologne and wears a black suit with a slim white tie.

"Hi, Al. You…Wow. You look nice." I'm trying to contain my utter surprise at how different he looks than he did a couple of weeks ago when I was first introduced to him in his dorm room. That day, he wore purple and black striped shorts, a black muscle shirt, and checkered high-top Vans. A skateboard sat beside him on the floor, and above his bed hung a freeway sign that said Speed Limit 69. I had thought to myself, *Who does this guy think he is?*

Now Al revs the engine again, and I step back in surprise. He chuckles, looking smitten. Even as the car idles, the deep buzz remains.

"Maybe I'll take you for a ride sometime." I glance inside the car and see black Recaro seats and an odd tank of some sort.

"What's that for?" I point to the console between the front and back seats.

"It's nitrous oxide—adds horsepower to the car." I have no idea what that means. I've never seen a car with anything like that inside it.

"You're dressed up. Where are you going?"

"It's Initiation Night tonight at my fraternity, Phi Kappa Tau. I'm getting my pin."

"Oh, great. Well, have fun."

"Yeah, okay. See ya."

He revs the engine twice more, winks at me, then burns a bit of rubber as he speeds away onto the streets of Chico. I can still hear those race-car rumbles of excitement as I walk through the double doors of the dorm. The attitude, the image, the force—I'm intrigued and oddly comforted by the strength of sound.

As the memory of my husband and me back in college fades, I unlock my car, get in, and turn the ignition key. The eerie quiet makes me jittery the entire drive home.

CHAPTER 4

LATE MARCH 1998

I've taken the day off work and am sitting in the waiting room at Kaiser Permanente. I'm fidgety in my seat, eager to see my doctor and find out what is wrong with me.

The nurse calls my name, but I don't hear it the first time. After an awkward pause of her holding the door open and staring at me, I finally figure it out and get up to follow her down the sterile hallway. I have no idea what she's saying during the usual routine of weigh in and blood pressure and temperature taking, and again rely on familiarity of where to stand or sit. After I follow her into the treatment room, she stands and looks at me as if she's waiting for a reply to a question I didn't catch. She gives me a sideways glance when I tell her I cannot hear.

Twenty minutes of sitting alone and staring at plain walls later, Dr. Holden enters with a rushed smile and an outstretched hand. I tell him about the pressure I feel in my right ear, the hum in my head, and not being able to hear out of either one of my ears. I am conscious of how irritating it is that he has one of those low tone male voices, which I'm realizing is the hardest for me to understand. I ask him to please speak louder and a bit slower as he recites a list of questions while I lean forward to listen. No, I don't have allergies or hay fever; no, I haven't recently had a cold or the flu; yes, I've tried taking Sudafed and Benadryl; no, I am not dizzy, off balance, or nauseous; and no, I haven't received a recent blow to the ear or been in the presence of loud blasts, equipment, or explosions. He ponders his scribbled notes for a few minutes and then looks up at me.

"I think you have labyrinthitis, Michele."

"Labyri-what?"

"Labyrinthitis. It's an inner ear infection that causes inflammation."

"So is there an antibiotic that I can take for it?" Even my own voice sounds foreign to me.

"Unfortunately, no. It's a viral infection. It has to run its course, I'm afraid."

"Umm, how long do you think it will… How long will I be like this?"

"Probably a month, maybe six weeks."

Did I just hear him right? No no. I couldn't have. "Could you repeat that?" I ask meekly. He does, and I feel my face heat up and a surge of adrenaline rush through my veins.

"But I…I don't…I can barely function like this! My job is all about communication and listening, and I don't know what I'm gonna do." I feel a rise of panic and tears begin filling my eyes. I rub them away with frustration. The doctor pretends not to notice.

"We can try a higher dose anti-inflammatory. If there isn't any improvement after about six weeks, I can refer you to an ear, nose, and throat specialist."

I can't believe I'm hearing what I'm hearing, while not hearing at the same time.

I leave his office, walking as fast as I can through the busy hallway of mumbles to the pharmacy for 80mg Motrin, and then through the parking lot to my car. I unlock the door of my BMW 740i, get in, slam the door shut as hard as I can, place my hands on the steering wheel, rest my forehead on top of it, and sob.

Three weeks later, there is still no change. It's raining on this early-April, Saturday morning while Al still sleeps. I'm standing at the front door, the screen held open with my hand. I'm straining to get closer to the drops. It's the first time in my life I can see rain falling, but cannot hear it. I see small pools accumulate on the large green leaves of the hydrangeas, and I'm wondering if the longer I stand here and listen, the more I will be able to will myself to hear. My eyes trail the surroundings to watch raindrops falling on familiar objects: the red brick planter box lining the covered porch, the black lamppost in the middle of the walkway, the base of the mature oak tree where its roots crack through the concrete driveway. I watch the drops fall, wait in suspense for that soothing, cleansing sound, but there's nothing. Stillness. Silence. I shake my head violently, as if to shake my hearing free from wherever it has gone.

Why is this happening? Why are my ears not working? Everything is quiet, yet my thoughts are loud.

Brennan taps me on the hand hanging by my side.

"The phone, Mommy. It's ringing," he says in his screechy, excited, three-year-old voice, which I've found is easier for me to hear due to the higher pitch and what I suspect is my maternal intuition. I pause for a moment and concentrate. I don't hear the phone. I know it is ringing, so I listen longer, more carefully, trying to manifest the sound of the ring. I walk to the corner of the kitchen and pick it up.

"Hello?"

I recognize my mother's English-accented voice, but I cannot understand anything she is saying. She is soft spoken, always has been, but it surprises me that all I hear on the line is a string of confusing mumbles.

"Mom," I interrupt, "I…I can't hear you very well at all. Can you speak louder?"

I push the handset harder into my right ear so it's pressing into my skull. I think I hear several words, but they don't make sense when I try to string them together: *boy…week….Sue?* Silence. I realize she is awaiting my response. I hesitate.

"Mom, something is wrong with my ears. I can't hear anything very well at all. It's been happening for a few weeks now. And I can't hear your voice right now over the phone. I have no idea what you just said. I'm…I'm sorry." The line goes quiet. Nothing.

"Michele? Michele?" My father's voice booms into the receiver.

"Dad! I can hear you!" I breathe a sigh of relief. It's not like he normally sounds, but his voice is so much easier for me in comparison. He's speaking louder.

"Mom was trying to talk to you but you can't hear her?" he seems perplexed, and I imagine his forehead with extra crinkled lines across it. I sigh. If it doesn't make sense to me, how will it make sense to anyone else?

I fill him in, tell him not to worry. That I've been to the doctor and have some weird virus that will supposedly run its course and go away soon. He lets me know that Mom was trying to tell me that they want to take the boys to the zoo this weekend and wondered if next Sunday morning around ten would work.

"That works great, Dad. Thanks. See you then." I'm eager to end the conversation.

I return the black handset to the receiver and close my eyes. Brennan must've been watching and listening the whole time because he walks over and hugs my leg. I bend down to stand on my knees, closer to his eye level.

"Do you want a hug, Mommy?" he asks as I follow his small perfectly shaped lips form the words and then land in an innocent smile.

"Yes," I mutter and nod at the same time. "I would really love that."

CHAPTER 5

MAY 1998

"I...I still can't hear you. Could you speak louder please and say it again?"

The young Asian man with glasses in a white lab coat delivers words like whispers. I strain to watch his lips, but his mouth opens only slightly when he talks, and I think he has an accent. Dr. Wong wheels his swivel stool closer to me.

"Did you experience any cold symptoms? Have you been exposed to loud noise?"

I shake my head no twice. I answered these same questions eight weeks ago. He picks up an otoscope hanging from the wall and motions for me to turn my head sideways. He inspects my ear canal and eardrum, then repeats this on the other side and furrows his brows. It feels overdone, like a ridiculous Saturday Night Live episode. *This man is the ear specialist?*

"I think we should schedule an MRI to rule out any tumor or

growth in your inner ear or your brain." He is easier to understand now that he is right next to me, and the words "tumor" and "brain" resound all too clearly.

"We will have your ears syringed out today to clear and clean out any possible obstructions from wax. And we will set up a complete audiogram, a full battery of hearing tests with the audiologist. I can review the results with you right afterwards."

While I watch his pen make notations on a page in a file folder, and wonder what these tests will show, images of my six-year-old self appear; and all of a sudden, I'm back there.

"It hurts, Mommy. It hurts really bad."

Tears move down both cheeks as I cup my hand over my left ear. For some reason, leaning into my hand or lying directly on the ear helps. While I've had other earaches before, this time, it feels like a spear was staked through my ear canal into the side of my brain.

"I know it does, sweetie," she says, nodding. "Hopefully, this will help."

Mom wraps a towel around a rubber hot water bottle and asks me to sit up for a minute. She places the bottle on my pillow, then smooths out the velour towel with her hand.

"Okay. Lie down on your left side." Her voice is soft and gentle.

As I feel the incoming warmth, I'm facing away from her, looking at the plain white wall of the motel room where we're staying for this summer family vacation in Palm Springs. We just got back from visiting the emergency room at Eisenhower

Medical Center. I have a severe ear infection in my left ear, and the doctor said there may be permanent damage to my hearing ability. The good news, as my mom explained it, is that my right ear is functioning well above the normal threshold and will compensate for my left.

I like feeling my mother's hand on my shoulder while her other hand strokes the teeny hairs on the side of my good ear. Comfort washes over me.

"How long will it hurt like this?" I move my knees in closer, curling up in a ball.

"I don't know. The medicine should help." Mom pats my back twice.

"Don't go, Mommy. I want you to stay."

"I'm not going anywhere. I'm right here."

She sits down on the side of my bed and continues to caress my hair, my right cheek, even down my neck. And as she does, I feel her hand temperature increase. I can smell her perfume, the scent she receives every Christmas from Dad: Estee Lauder's Youth Dew. I scoot over to give her more room, and a couple of moments later, I feel her lie down behind me. She's facing my same way, her arm draped over mine. I long to stay wrapped in this moment of safety and security forever.

As the memory fades, and I come back to sitting in the doctor's office, I realize I've adapted to not hearing well out of my left ear for twenty-six years. I've always known to turn my head and receive whispers with my right ear, but other than that, I've not been inconvenienced; and it's just second nature. My left-ear deficit has gone generally unnoticed, just as the doctor in Palm Springs predicted. Until now.

I walk down the stark medical center hallway to another waiting room I've never entered before. Audiology. A large sign on the wall near the receptionist's window says, "If you are worried that you will not hear your name called, please notify the receptionist." I hadn't realized how much I actually had been worrying about this until now. I wait in line behind an elderly man wearing a brown cardigan sweater, holding a cane, but that's not the most noticeable thing about him. It's the bulky skin-colored contraptions that rest behind his ears with opaque tubes coming out of them. I look quickly around, summing up my surroundings. I am out of place. I am the youngest in the room by far, except for a little boy, probably four years old, who is playing beside a lowered table with a colorful pile of Legos on it. I choose a seat close to him with a clear view of the door. When my name is called, I do hear it, but I wonder if it is because every time the door opens, I intently watch her lips move when she speaks. Matching the moving lips to the sounds, watching for the connection, helps me understand the words. I realize it's how I've "heard" my name, and that I'm already compensating for my hearing loss.

I am led into a small square soundproof room. The audiologist wearing a white lab coat, *A. Turietta* embroidered above the left side pocket, introduces herself as Analissa. She looks directly at me when she speaks. She has shoulder-length brown curly hair and a gentle-natured smile that I find immediately comforting—a far cry from Dr. Wong. I imagine she is in her early thirties too, like me, but that thought also brings up some sadness. I never thought I would be thirty-two years old and unable to hear.

Analissa instructs me to sit in the straight-backed chair, place the headphones over my ears, and wait for instructions. She slowly over-enunciates each syllable she speaks to me, but it's a relief that I can hear what she is saying. She turns and leaves, securing the thick vault-type door behind her. I don't as much hear the sound of it shut as much as I feel it. *Thud.* It feels like I'm being held in a padded cell, locked out of the normal world. The only visible window is a small one behind which she appears and gives me instructions. It intensifies the separateness and aloneness that I've felt since I lost my ability to hear, and my composure is threatened. I want to roll my eyes at myself. When will my about-to-cry-ness stop?

"Michele, can you hear me?" she asks at a reasonable volume level through my headset.

"Yes," I answer.

"The first battery of tests we will do involve sounds in your right ear. If you can place your right elbow on the arm of the chair, each time you hear a beep, please raise your index finger to indicate a sound, okay?"

"Okay," I reply, my right fist ready to respond.

I hear a beep and raise my finger, then another beep, a pause, another beep—I think, although it is a completely different tone than the one before. As I continue to concentrate, I hear various tones, different volume levels, sequences of beeps followed by lulls of void. There are times when I am not sure if there is really a beep or if I'm imagining one. Again, I think I hear one. Didn't I? I question myself on raising my finger or not, and quickly decide it is better to raise it and be wrong than to not raise it as if I didn't hear anything. After a while, Analissa's voice returns to my headset and tells me it's time to switch to the left ear. This one is much harder for me to listen with, but I use the same strategies, raising my left finger anytime I think I've heard a tone.

Another round of tests begins. This time, she informs me that beeps will be served to both ears in no particular order, and again, instructs me to raise a finger to identify on which side I hear a sound. Midway through, she walks in the heavy door and places a metal vibrating device to the bone behind my ear, mentioning something about bone conduction, which is as foreign to me as all these assessments. I feel confused in a dizzying kind of way, and I'm getting tired from concentrating and listening so hard. I want it to be over.

She returns to remove the piece on my skull, and I'm willing her to tell me we are finished. Instead, *thud*. She locks me in again. When I see her through the glass, her voice fills my ears with the update that she will add in a "distortion noise" for this next part of the test. Now I must identify beeps within a sort of overwhelming wind tunnel of whooshing noises. I hear a series of beeps until they register and prompt the raise-a-finger response three times in a row. Long pauses with no beeps follow and make me nervous. There must be some tones mixed in, and I am just not hearing them. I sigh. Tears are on standby again. My heart is beating faster, and I feel a strong desire to flee. Analissa must've noticed.

"We are almost done, Michele, but we have one more to complete." She continues to exaggerate her enunciation. "Repeat the word back to me that I say in your ear, okay?"

I nod and listen for the word. Two syllable words are given first at a volume I can hear and understand. But my confident replies don't last long. As the words get harder to hear, I sense my brain piecing bits together.

"Toothbrush," I reply after hearing "brush" and considering what would go in front of it. I have no choice but to guess, but it's excruciating to try to hear something that I cannot hear. The volume decreases steadily until it sounds like Analissa is drifting away from me. I notice my chest tighten. By the time I am given the one-syllable words, I am stumped. I sit in uncomfortable silence wanting to respond, but I have no idea if the given word was "there," "air," "bear," "dare," or "fair." Again, all I can do is guess, hoping that I am right.

32

The longer this goes on though, the more defeated I feel. I have no idea what she is saying, and I'm tired of guessing. It's now the third time I have to respond the same way: "Umm, I…I… don't…know," and I cannot take it anymore. My elbow resting on the arm of the chair, I place my hand on my forehead and bow my head in surrendered failure. My tears fall fast.

When Analissa opens the door, she walks over and places her hand gently on my shoulder. She invites me to follow her into her office and take a chair next to hers. Looking directly into my eyes and speaking slowly, enunciating every word at a good volume, she shares the news.

"Your hearing ability is in the severe hearing loss range," she explains with compassion, showing me a chart of where normal lies and where my scores fall. She points out my left hearing ability in comparison with my right and confirms the likely irreparable nerve damage in my left ear from childhood. Her chart shows my right hearing level plummeting in its direction, south of normal. She explains why I have difficulty functioning as a result, noting that in some hearing thresholds, I am not hearing anything. Low tones in particular, like men's voices. She explains that consonant sounds of *f, s, sh, th, t, p, k, ch,* and *n* are particularly challenging for me to decipher, whereas vowels are easier. I listen and feel more understood than I have in weeks, but what-ifs quickly flood my mind.

"Do you know what the cause is?" Analissa inquires with a gentle dose of care evident from her warm eyes.

"No," I reply, nodding and wiping tears from my cheeks and beneath my nose. "There doesn't seem to be any cause or reason. I just woke up one day like this. It doesn't make any sense."

"Mommy. Mommy!"

I gradually begin to feel the push of fingers against my shoulder and turn over to see Brennan standing at my bedside. When my eyes focus enough to look into his, I see he is crying.

"Are you okay?" I ask as I move over, closer to him.

He mumbles something back that I can't hear and then falls into my chest. He says more that I can't decipher, so I gently lift his head up and away to look directly at him and watch his mouth.

"Say that again."

"I…had…a…bad dream. I was calling you. Why didn't you come?" he says as pools of tears fall from the whites of his brown eyes, and his sobs get louder.

A thick lump forms in my throat.

"I'm sorry, sweetie. You can always come down and wake me up and tell me, okay?" I stroke his cheek and watch his lips again.

"But sometimes, I'm scared. Of the dark. And you…you didn't hear me."

His expression of utter shock and disappointment bites me hard. I wish he knew how paralyzed I feel by that same frustration and angst.

I open my side of the bedcovers and pat the sheets, inviting him to lie beside me. He nods and smiles, climbs up, and allows me to wrap my arms around his little three-year-old body.

Later this same morning, while getting ready for work, I talk with Al.

"I hate not being able to hear them at night. I feel like a bad mother." I'm standing behind the sink on my side, putting mascara on while looking at his lips through the mirror.

"Well, I didn't hear him last night either," he says after brushing his teeth.

"If you do hear them calling for me, will you wake me up right away, please?"

"Sure. But I'm just sayin'. My ears aren't broken and I didn't hear him last night either."

He dries his mouth on the hanging towel, gives me a closed mouth half grin, and turns to leave the room.

I sigh and suppose he said that to make me feel better, but it doesn't. I want him to tell me he understands how much I'm struggling with not being able to hear and that everything will turn out okay. I can't shake my worry. All the what-ifs start scrolling through my mind again: *What if there's an intruder and my boys yell for me? Or they are sick, throwing up and calling for help? Or they smell smoke from a fire? Oh my God. What if they scream and I don't come because…I can't…hear them?*

I feel as though I need to roar a dragon's breath of fire because the doctors have no fucking answers. All I got from the appointment with the specialist was head nods and lip puckers of utter disbelief, and a prescription for prednisone. I am starting to hate the aloneness I feel. Even here at home with Al. The separation and isolation. The fear and worry. In hating all of these things, in small ways, I am beginning to hate myself.

It's 1973. My brother, Mark, and I stand facing my dad. He's on his knees, both arms outstretched, displaying a mischievous grin of challenge.

"Try to get to the front doors," he initiates with confidence, moving side to side, wearing tennis shorts and sneakers like a goaltender defending his net.

Mark looks at me with toothless grin full of desire. He covers the side of his mouth with his hand and stands on his tippy toes to whisper in my left ear. As he begins to speak, I turn my head to give him my right ear instead. I whisper back to Mark the directive to rush at the same time, each of us past one of dad's arms. After a quick nod to signal our start, we charge. Mark is caught easily in his eagerness. Squeals of laughter fill high ceilings of the entryway while he's tickled on his stomach and side.

"Help!" he pleads, still laughing.

My attempt to move past my dad's left arm is thwarted by an equal gate-type restraint. Both Mark and I are captured in a sandwich hold. We're both squirming to avoid tickle torture, letting out screams and screeches of painful delight. Monster Games as we call it. Our favorite game with Dad.

Mark and I work as a team to pry fingers from our waists and escape capture by backing up and attempting again to distract Dad enough to make a clear run for victory. We take a deep breath when we've freed ourselves from the monster and prepare for round two.

"Let's go!" Sure enough, we're recaptured, this time with Mark in the scissor hold between Dad's outstretched and crossed legs, and me struggling for success. I reach behind Dad, only to be grabbed by my calf and tickled on the bottom of my foot—the worst tickle spot of all. Five- and seven-year-old shrieks, moans, and cries of "Okay, okay. Stop. Okay" mix with laughter while Dad makes the *Grrrrrr* of monster power. All three of us are intertwined, breathing hard at our efforts to win, when all of a sudden, Dad releases Mark and me. We watch his solemn gaze shift up to the top of the landing, so we turn and look too.

My mother stares down on us, her pale porcelain face expressionless and makeup free. Jet-black strands of pillow head hair meet the nape of her long navy-blue housecoat. Only the skin from the top of her neck up is visible.

"Could you pl-eeeeea-se keep it down?" She squints her eyes almost shut while she speaks. Her tone is emphatic and exasperated. There is no smile.

"Oh yes. Umm, yes," my father replies, studying her the entire time.

Saying nothing more, she turns around and slowly takes three steps back into the darkness she appeared from. The shut of her bedroom door is especially loud in the newfound silence following so much laughter. Mark and I look at Dad. More silence. Eventually, he says, "Okay. That's enough, guys. Game's over."

He stands up, brushes off his knees, forces a half smile, and walks toward his record player.

CHAPTER 6

JUNE 1998

I wake up every day hoping to hear again.

The first thing I do is say something out loud. I remember how my voice should sound. Yet every morning, I don't recognize the sound of myself.

I start to notice a new tiredness. Throughout the day, my brain works hard to concentrate on the words delivered to me, trying to connect sounds and understand their accurate meaning. But still, I'm missing a lot of conversations; I know I am. I nod a lot, smile, and say, "Uh-huh," or even chuckle a bit, all in an effort to avoid saying to people, "I'm sorry. I am hearing impaired. I can't hear what you're saying very well."

The boys are tucked in and asleep. I walk upstairs and see Al sitting on the black leather couch, looking at the television, remote in his hand. He mumbles something.

"What was that? I, uh, didn't hear you." As I walk toward him, he speaks again. I miss the meaning again.

"I…look…I still didn't hear that."

"I said, 'DO YOU WANT TO WATCH A MOVIE WITH ME?'" His tone pierces the air and confuses me.

"Al, I don't…I don't need you to yell at me. I… Can't you just look directly at me and slow down when you speak so I can follow along better?"

He rolls his eyes and groans, "Do you have any idea what my day at work was like? Everything I had to put up with? Now all I want to do is watch a movie and relax, and you're getting on my case. Now I don't even speak right."

"No, I'm not. I…I just wanted you to know—" He cuts me off by turning the volume up and staring into the screen.

I want to curl up in a ball and disappear. Escape the aloneness. The isolation. The confusion. The shame. The frustration. I wish it would all go away.

I'm sitting on the paper-protected table, waiting for Dr. Wong of the ear, nose, and throat department again. He's going to review my second battery of hearing tests. He enters the room, washes his hands, and sits on the stool facing me. His eyebrows merge as he looks down at paperwork. I focus on his lips, waiting for them to move.

"Your hearing is not improving. In fact, it's getting worse.

The prednisone didn't help at all." I have to give him credit; he's a straight shooter.

"Why would that be?" my voice cracks.

"I don't know," he says, shaking his head back and forth. "I think I will refer you to Neurology. I'm not convinced this is ear-related."

"But what? You mean like a nervous system problem? What would cause that?

"I'm not sure. I think we should consider every avenue."

"But is there anything I can do in the meantime? I mean, it's been months now. I...I need help functioning in the world better. Especially at work. My job is all about communication."

"Uh, you can probably borrow an assistive listening device. It's called a Pocket Talker. It might help."

I can't picture in my mind what he is referring to, but I ask where I go to get one. At this point, I'm willing to try anything that might help me hear.

"You can get one down the street at the Kaiser Hearing Center. I'll have staff give you the address along with an appointment in Neurology, and then another appointment with me after that." Dr. Wong stands up and extends his hand.

Walking through the halls and down the escalator of the large sterile medical center, I glance down at two slips of paper in my hand: one for my next appointment in two weeks with the neurologist, and the other for a follow-up appointment with Dr. Wong the day after. I focus on my frustration at receiving no answers about why this is happening. Why is it taking the doctors this long to figure it out and find a cure?

Soon, I'm standing at the counter of the hearing center in front of a large lady with glasses and no smile. I'm wondering before I've spoken if I'll have trouble hearing her. This is how my brain works now.

"Can I help you?" I hear her better than I thought I would, and am beginning to realize that one-on-one close proximity communication is the easiest for me.

"My doctor sent me here to borrow a Pocket Talker or assistive listening device," I say, offering a smile that doesn't alter her expression at all. She turns and picks up a battery-pack-type device with a fairly long cord, and a headset with ear buds. She lays them on the counter in front of me. My eyes widen. It looks like an ugly and bulky Walkman, designed to be worn on a belt or held in the hand. The base includes an acorn-sized microphone. I have never seen one of these before and have no idea how it is supposed to work.

"Um, can you please show me how this works and how to use it?"

"Is this for you?" she asks, emphasizing the question mark and creasing her brow.

"Yes. I...I'm not able to hear very well right now." Just admitting that sends me close to tears, but I don't think she notices. She unwraps the cord, points to the microphone, and tells me that when on, this will amplify words; and wearing the headset, I'll receive the sounds. She points to a volume control and says nothing more.

I decide against trying it on right there. I want to leave. So I pick it up, thank her, turn, and walk back out to my car. Sitting with air conditioning blasting, I look up at myself in the rearview mirror. I place the headset on my head and hold the microphone in my hand. Thoughts scream through my mind. *Won't people think I'm listening to a CD or something if I wear this around? Doesn't this look more like I'm shutting people's voices out instead of seeking them? Why does it have to be so intrusive and ugly? How will I look when I'm wearing this in a suit? Will it even make any difference?*

I take it off, toss it on the seat beside me, and drive home.

After I've picked up the boys from school and day care and served them a snack, I sit down in the living room, decide to look at the device again, and try it out. Brennan immediately asks me about it. As I position the headphones on my head and turn it on, I tell him I'm hoping it will help me hear him and his brother better.

"Helloooooo. Hello, Mama. Helloooooo!" he shouts into the microphone I'm holding. The sound in my ears feels like blasts of excruciating pain. I rush to turn the volume way down in hopes it just needs an adjustment to work better. Brennan begins to run around the room then rush back at the microphone, shouting words and noises, as if it's some kind of toy. Trevor, who's eleven months old and already walking, follows his brother. They run, scream, and laugh, practically piercing my eardrums with every high-pitched shriek.

"Stop it! Just stop it, Brennan!" I don't intend to yell my frustration and annoyance, but I do. He stops and stares at me in complete confusion.

"Why?"

"Because when you shout into it, it…it hurts."

I realize then, as his little soon-to-be four-year-old face looks up at me wearing a strange headset, that this contraption makes no sense to him either. I sigh and remove it.

"I'm sorry. Do you want to try it out and see what it's like?"

He nods and smiles, adding a little hop. I place and adjust

the headset on him, show him the volume button, and place the microphone base in his hand to hold. He walks away from me, talking into it and listening to his own voice, smiling and giggling. I watch and listen, wishing I could hear exactly what Brennan is saying. I smile and glance over at Trevor studying his brother's every move. Until I'm interrupted by a terrifying thought: *what if I'm not able to hear Trevor's voice and the first words he speaks?*

1972

"Wait. Don't let go yet!"

I try to find balance as I pedal. My hands clench the pink handle bar grips while Daddy holds on to the silver handle on the back of my white seat.

"You're doing great," he says as he runs alongside me in his blue shirt, shorts, and tennis shoes.

"I'm scared, Daddy!"

"You'll be fine."

Unsure of my ability and worried about no longer having training wheels on my bicycle, I want to know I won't fall. I want to be sure. I hear his footsteps against the asphalt of our cul-de-sac get faster and faster.

"I don't know if I can do it."

"You're already doing it!"

"What?" I see him still running beside me.

"You're riding on your own now. I'm not holding on anymore." He holds up both hands.

My mouth hangs open in delight. I pedal and laugh, and don't want to stop. Dad takes a break from running and claps. When I turn around and come back down the street, my brother Mark claps, and jumps up and down on the green lawn of our front yard.

"I'm riding a two-wheeler, Mark!"

I continue up the whole length of the short street and back again several times. When I steer toward the driveway, Dad rushes up to tell me to back pedal to stop, and helps me stabilize and place my feet on the ground.

"Can I do it again?"

"Of course. This time, I will just give you a little push. Keep pedaling."

As the wheels turn, my confidence surges. I feel the air brushing against my skin and meet real freedom maybe for the first time in my short life. When I arrive back at the same spot I'd started from, I practice a successful stop. Daddy and Mark clap and cheer for me again.

I stay straddled over the frame and glance over at the front door of our house.

"I want Mommy to see me ride."

"She…well, next time she will."

"But can't you go get her?"

"She's not feeling good. She's lying down. Let's not disturb her, okay?"

She's been lying down a lot lately. I don't understand. I think about whether or not I should say what I'm feeling.

"I just…I wish she was here too."

I decide to try the Pocket Talker out at work and make a goal to put it to use with more than one person before the school year ends. Both secretaries in the school office know I've been to frequent medical appointments and listen to my updates with compassion. Standing in a dark-green pantsuit, I share with them my need to see if this listening device will help me. Even just placing the headset over my head elicits feelings of vulnerability and being different.

I turn the device to a low volume first and nod. After asking Christy to read something aloud to see how well I can listen, I also hear the office door opening and closing, the phone ringing, and the rustling of papers on Betty's desk. All of these sounds I've been missing layer on top of each other. When two teachers enter and add their voices into the mix, I get completely overwhelmed. After not being able to hear much of anything for months, it suddenly sounds like everything and everyone are yelling at me. I take off the device and let out an exasperated sigh. I don't want to use it. What this device amplifies most for me is my loneliness. I'd rather hone my lip-reading skills and fumble through conversations than feel alone in a roomful of screams.

I've had some conversations with individual teachers who have shown great compassion for me and my hearing loss. I'm realizing that pretending to hear words when I haven't doesn't work, and my communication skills are diminishing. As the school year comes to a close, I share at a staff meeting of twenty-five teachers that I am still struggling with not being able to hear well and that the doctors have found no known causes. I feel a lump arrive in my throat as I explain that large group situations are the most challenging for me.

"It's difficult for me to identify where sounds or voices are coming from. In other words, I may hear something being said, but I'm not sure who's saying it. Additionally, I'm learning that if people slow down their speech and enunciate clearly, I can hear them a bit better."

As I speak, I feel a rawness inside. I wonder if I'll be able to hold it together when I notice several teachers in the room nodding gently and raising a tissue to moist eyes. When my own unusual public tears emerge, I decide to be even more honest.

"This is tough for me emotionally as well as physically. I so appreciate and need your patience and understanding. My hope is that everything will sort itself out over the summer, and I'll be fine by the time we all return in the fall."

When the teachers leave the lounge and return to their classrooms, I feel their genuine support, yet somehow still feel achingly alone.

July 6, 1973

I'm seven years old. I think I hear my white cat, Angel, meowing. She's been missing. I run downstairs to the kitchen, hoping to see her near her food bowl. I peek my head into the laundry room where I watch the back of my mother reaching into the washer to put whites in the dryer.

"Mommy, is Angel back yet?"

"No, I still haven't seen her." She turns around to face me, her blue eyes misty.

"I thought I heard her."

My mom turns back around.

Two hours later, as the San Gabriel Valley heat begins to wane, Mom asks if I want to come with her to look for Angel. She suggests we get in the car and drive around the nearby streets and cul-de-sacs. I nod my head and follow her through the garage door, which has already been lifted open. I slide in the long front seat of her blue Chevy Impala. As she turns the key and starts the engine, with her other hand, she grabs the knob to roll down her window. She gestures for me to do the same on my side. As we back out of the driveway into the cul-de-sac of about twelve homes, Mom's head swivels on her shoulders.

"Look around everywhere. We'll call her name too, okay? Ain-gel…Ain-gel…"

I copy her tone of voice and amplify it. She has never spoken very loudly, and I'm worried that Angel might not be able to hear her. I figure if she says it and I follow, maybe our chances will be better.

The car moves slowly down the residential streets surrounding our house. We scour driveways, the asphalt in front of us, grassy front lawns, and even underneath parked cars along the curbs. Near the end of the street, we turn around and do the same as we travel back the same path. We call her name over and over. I sit up on my knees to get a better view out the window as the summer breeze teases my pigtails. We've looked down three different streets so far.

"Angel. Ain-gel…Ain—" my voice cracks at the third one. I envision Angel's emerald eyes and the jeweled collar my mom bought her that matched them. Where is she?

"Mommy, why can't we find her? Where did she go?"

"Cats don't like loud noises. The Fourth of July fireworks and firecrackers may have scared her. She could've run away." She reaches over and grabs my hand.

"Run away? But to where? Why didn't she just come home?" My eyes fill up as I search her face for reason. She says nothing and nods her head back and forth in slow motion.

"I don't know, Michele. I'm sorry."

When we pull back into our driveway and get out of the car, I want us to do more to find Angel.

"Let's walk around and look more," I plead.

"I think we looked everywhere we could."

"But, we haven't found her yet."

I don't want Mom to just walk back in the house as though everything is okay when it's not.

I wonder if Angel is alone and afraid. I wonder if she is trying to find us. I wonder if she is lying somewhere, hurt or injured. I walk away from our front yard into the middle of the street and turn my head in every direction.

"Ain-gel. Ain-gel. Ain-gel."

I want to yell loud enough so she can hear me wherever she is. My eyes burn. I want to stomp my feet and pound my fists against something, but all I do is stand there in utter defeat and sob.

How can something so precious to me just all of a sudden be gone?

CHAPTER 7

November 2014

While we continue to sail through calm seas, I'm sitting in the Sea Adventurer's library on the fourth floor of the ship, waiting for the start of our Trekker Safety Meeting. The room is quiet, if not totally inviting, filled with bolted-down wooden tables. Three of the tables have checkerboards or chessboards painted on them to help passengers whittle away the hours. Shelves of bookcases line the walls. Every shelf is marked with a white label, notating a different country in alphabetical order, and I can't think of any exclusions. There are two computer stations off to one side and two dark-brown fabric couches with pressure marks that face each other in the center of the room. Folding chairs have been positioned in a circle for the five of us non-skiers. So far, we haven't acknowledged each other beyond nervous smiles as we sit and wait in anticipation, hands folded in our laps.

Sarah, our guide for the week, enters the room with her long wavy black hair pulled back in a ponytail, looking at ease in jeans and a turquoise long-sleeve shirt. I'd met her two days before in the lobby of the Hotel Albatross in Ushuaia, where she approached me with a white piece of paper folded in her hand.

"Hi, I saw you sitting here and thought we could go over your equipment."

Sarah's smile is warm and bright. She stands to my right and suggests we go through a list of items one by one so she can check them off. She unfolds her paper carefully. I notice her short unpainted nails before she looks down at me and begins.

"Layered clothing and waterproof outerwear? Waterproof boots suitable for hiking? Snowshoes? Harness? A carabiner that locks? Uh, an avalanche transceiver?"

I nod in response to each item on her checklist, which makes me chuckle to myself. Two months ago, I had never heard of some of these things. I tell her honestly that I'm not sure yet if I will actually be trekking on glaciers and snow-covered mountains, and that I've never done it before. In fact, I don't even understand exactly what trekking is. Sarah assures me that it is fully my choice to participate, but reminds me that it's only a possibility if I have all of the necessary equipment.

"Okay. How about a shovel and a probe?"

I shake my head sheepishly. Gordon is out on nearby Martial Glacier with his ski group, practicing how to skin up in Antarctica. Without him nearby to consult, I feel unprepared for all these questions. My expression must be noticeable because she points out right away that it's not a requirement to have these. I'm half listening to her elaborate on why she would like to find out if anyone else in our group is carrying them, while thinking about how even the remote possibility of falling into a crevasse or being caught in an avalanche terrifies me. My eyes flit about the room at all the people showing off their gear, eager for Sarah's attention. Sarah clears her throat and glances down at her paper again.

"One more quick question. Do you have an ice axe?" I look up at her, and she grins, walking away, knowing my response before I utter an answer.

Now Sarah's in front of me again, still radiating health and confidence. I shoot her a nervous smile as she goes around the room facilitating introductions. There's Marese from Sydney, Australia, who makes warm eye contact with everyone and exudes enthusiasm; Katy from San Diego, California, who's athletic, fit, and the youngest in our group; Monica from Stockholm, Sweden, who says she's trekked many times before but wants to apologize for not speaking English well; and Judy from Denver, Colorado, who reminds me of what my mother might look like at seventy years of age if she was adventurous and passionate about living life. All of us have husbands who will ski while we trek, but only Judy and I have never trekked before.

Sarah stands in the center of our circle.

"Let's take out our avalanche transceivers and turn them on. You will see a lighted LED screen that displays the level of battery life." Judy and I look around at the others, hoping to learn how this is done, but soon realize that all the beacons are different makes and models. I finally find the correct side button, push it, and watch a green glow emerge with a battery icon showing 95 percent. My hand feels shaky just holding this bulky, rectangular, radio-type device that fills the entire palm of my hand.

"Now please place your transceiver in 'search' mode." I hear a succession of high-pitched beeps every second from my device and everyone else's.

"You hear these life-saving sounds now because your transceivers are picking up the signal of mine in send mode. Notice the changes in sound as I get closer, then farther away from you and what the screen says as you move it around."

Sarah walks toward each of us and then backs away. Listening for louder, more rapid bleeps while pointing this contraption in various directions makes me feel like I'm aboard the Star Trek Enterprise using the Universal Translator.

She continues to teach, "You will be able to tell if you are close or farther away to a victim buried beneath the snow by looking at the number on your screen. You want to move fast and watch the number get smaller, like this: point seven, point four, point three. It allows us to locate the area to use our shovel and probe for a rescue." Sarah finishes her demonstration by showing us how to switch to send mode, which is what we will do when getting dressed to go out, using a strap to position the beacon under a couple layers of clothes against our chest.

"How long do we have to find and dig someone out?" Marese asks with her Australian accent. My heartbeat increases when Sarah hesitates and then answers, "Five minutes."

I swallow and take in a slow deep breath.

Next, Sarah guides us each through putting our harness around our hips and attaching a locking carabiner. I listen to the clinks and clacks of safety from this small but heavy piece of climbing equipment that will supposedly hold my body weight. Trekking in these conditions means we will be locked together on a roped line, walking single file in case one of us falls into a crevasse. I feel heat rising through my bloodstream. I'm afraid. Afraid of being trapped in a narrow crack in the glacier, stuck for who knows how long in the silent unknown.

One day later, the ship's first anchor plunges into an open sea full of what looks like floating white popcorn pieces. It's light at four in the morning after just a few hours of darkness when I take my first peek out our stateroom window. Icebergs jut out in every direction, each of them unique in size, shape, and height. Humongous mountains in the distance are fully covered in ice and snow. I touch the window and feel the bitter chill. There are no structures, no vegetation, no colors besides the blue sky and ocean. We've arrived along the Antarctic Peninsula at Chiriguano Bay, just outside Gerlache Strait.

A morning announcement over the loud speaker directs skiers to gather after breakfast for departure downstairs, properly dressed for the first skiing expedition. After all skiers have departed, the trekkers will go out. In our stateroom, I watch Gordon add layer after layer of clothing along with his avalanche beacon, as if he does this every day. He smiles at me several times while I marvel at the eagerness on his face.

"You look excited and ready to go."

"I am, baby! Today's the day I've been looking forward to for months. Come downstairs with me and grab the camera. I want you to take a picture of me with my group."

On the third floor at a holding area near an exit, I watch group after group pile up skis, backpacks, and poles. I hear the clinks of carabiners dangling from harnesses, and watch guides tie ice axes together in a bundle. Skiers wait in eagerness to board Zodiacs in groups of ten. Gordon flashes me a thumbs up when his group is called to depart. Bundled up in his helmet, goggles, and gloves, he blows me a kiss, fastens his life jacket, and steps down a set of temporary metal stairs where two guides help each passenger board and sit on the edge of the little rubber boat. I take photos as Gordon and nine others motor away from the ship until they look like a piece of dark chocolate floating in the distance. I say a silent prayer.

A couple hours later, ninety-seven passengers have left to ski so the five of us "trekkers" are finally called to board. I sit on the edge of the sturdy rubber boat, staring at the rare spectacular blue emanating from the iceberg where it meets the surface of the water. The milky turquoise spreads like a film glowing from below, and I am mesmerized. I wonder about hidden depths below, and my heart begins thumping beneath my layers of protective clothing. Sea ice crackles as our driver and naturalist Christian stands at the back of the boat, one hand around a long steering handle, navigating us away from the safety of the expedition ship. I glance around at icebergs everywhere and notice how the vibrant sunshine makes white snow whiter, stark against the background of a cloudless sky. I smell frigid air with no odor whatsoever. There's no garbage, no pollution, no evidence of land mammals. This does not look to me as terrain to touch. I feel as if I have been transported to another planet.

None of us five trekkers say a word. The Zodiac glides through the water with grace, crunching through sections of ice toward a tall, wide, snow-covered mountain. Cracks, ridges, and one long slope of thick white smoothness covers the dark rocks below. The group lets out a few whispered "wows." Looking up, I feel like I'm staring at a spectacular cathedral. Beauty and wonder exist here, yet a sense of harshness and danger lurk under the surface. Silent, serene, and empty, yet full of sharp ridges, cracks, and untraveled unknowns.

I spot the inchworm-like lines of five or six specks each, climbing up the mountain, spread out in various sections. They look like dot-to-dots along the quiet white ice. They are skiers, my husband included, roped together in small groups and making their first ascent to the summit where they will meet their reward of skiing down.

As we pull up to the landing area, my chest tightens and my legs feel shaky. I am worried that I will fall through a snow-bridged crevasse—a deep wedge-shaped opening on a glacier that's invisible because a thin layer of snow forms on top of it. I'm convinced that I will fall through, be swallowed up, and trapped if I participate in the trekking excursion. My throat closes tight, but my voice is able to squeak out my feelings to our guide anyway.

"Uh, Sarah, I…I am not going to go after all. I can't do it yet. This just feels…I-I-I am just overwhelmed by all of this." Sarah nods and smiles with genuine compassion. Marese, who's sitting beside me, puts a hand on my knee then pats it gently.

I watch as Sarah exits first onto the edge of the glacier and asks us to toss her the backpacks and ropes. The four other trekkers follow carefully and look back at me with smiles and waves. I feel a tinge of loneliness at not belonging as the Zodiac backs away.

Now it's just me in the boat with Christian. He suggests that we cruise around a bit and take in the scenery, perhaps even find some penguins. I get my camera ready. Icebergs are everywhere I look. I study the complex and pristine exposed sections with their soft curves as well as jagged edges. From the base of each iceberg, a halo of turquoise shine emanates from the mixture of ice and seawater. But as we drift past, it's what lies beneath the surface that intrigues me most. The other two-thirds: unseen, unpredictable, and forever hidden from knowing. I think about myself, my experiences—my own image of shiny and bright, with the dark unvarnished parts hidden deep below.

At one point, Christian cuts the engine so we just float. The only sound is the crackle and pops of sea ice. I listen with my whole body and realize I'm hearing the purest sound—desolate nature. Consumed by awe, my eyes fill with grateful tears. Memories of a different kind of remote silence and separateness flood my mind.

CHAPTER 8

JUNE 1998

I'm in yet another department of the Kaiser Medical Center, sitting in front of Dr. Igra, a neurologist. He's a large seasoned man with white hair, white bushy eyebrows, and thick glasses. With his pen in hand, he asks for the same history of events I've told to every other doctor. Aren't all these facts documented in my medical records? Dr. Igra is not easy to hear, and I'm beginning to think all male doctors have no idea how to speak to a hearing-impaired patient. I wonder for the first time if I'm going to need to look into learning sign language this summer. And then I wonder how that works with family. Will my kids need to learn it too?

A knock on my knee halts my thought. Dr. Igra checks all my reflexes, looks into my eyes with a blindingly bright light, watches me walk a straight line from both in front of and behind, and asks me to follow a series of verbal commands.

"Close your eyes and open your mouth, touch your left ear and stick out your tongue, raise your right knee and clap." I make all the motions and know I've been successful in hearing his commands.

He reaches into a large manila envelope, reveals film of the recent MRI of my brain, and places it on a lighted board on the wall in front of us. I am relieved to hear him say I have no brain tumor and no acoustic neuroma. A silent pause lingers as he flips through pages in a file on his desk. He clears congestion from his throat, shakes his head side to side, and looks at me.

"This is not a neurological issue. You are a very healthy thirty-two-year-old female. This is an ear disturbance." I feel a rush of relief, but it's mixed with lingering frustration. *How long will it take doctors to figure this out?*

He refers me back to ENT.

During my visit with Dr. Wong the following day, he shakes his head in frustration at my most recent hearing test assessment.

"Your hearing has stabilized in the severe hearing loss range, meaning, there is no fluctuation. Given the lack of improvement, you're not going to be happy with my prognosis." He looks down at his folder instead of at me.

"Uh, okay. I… What is it?"

"My diagnosis is sudden sensorineural hearing loss with no known cause. It's idiopathic. I believe the inner ear or nerve pathways between the inner ear and your brain have been damaged. Maybe by a viral infection, neurological condition, or autoimmune problem. We don't know. But the longer your ability to hear is compromised, the less chance of improvement. I suggest you get fitted for hearing aids as soon as possible."

I'm spinning through all his long words and am not sure I've heard him right.

"Hearing aids? But wait. Does this mean my hearing won't come back?"

"The longer this goes on, the less likely that is."

This sentence of permanent solitude rattles me. I'm left speechless while noisy thoughts flow through my mind. *What is life going to be like if I can't ever hear again? What about my little boys? Will I feel this alone forever?*

I begin to sob while Dr. Wong looks at me with a blank face. His stoic presence only makes me cry harder, until I'm almost hyperventilating and the only sound coming out of me is wails.

After tucking the boys into bed, I grab my Dell laptop while Al's watching television and type in a search for sudden hearing loss. I'm looking for someone like me. Or maybe I'm looking for me; I don't know. I search several sites and read lists of explanations, symptoms, and causes; but my case doesn't exactly match any of the scenarios described. I sit shaking my head and repeatedly sighing in exasperation. Most of the causes of sudden loss of hearing are due to disease, trauma, or old age if not linked to congenital or genetic conditions. A high percentage of people with sudden hearing loss also experience dizziness or vertigo, which doesn't apply to me either. I read through diseases and disorders that I've been tested for with negative results: acoustic neuroma, meningitis, mumps, measles, syphilis, and meningioma. As I quickly scan the page for

Sudden Sensorineural Hearing Loss (SSHL), several sections catch my attention: "Only 10 to 15 percent of cases diagnosed as SSHL have an identifiable cause. The majority of evidence points to some type of inflammation in the inner ear as the most common cause," and "About half of people with SSHL will recover some or all of their hearing spontaneously, usually within one to two weeks of onset." One to two weeks? I sigh as though I've been holding my breath. I keep reading, and the final words jump out as if written in bold: "**The worse the hearing loss, the poorer the prognosis for recovery. SSHL is the most common type of permanent hearing loss.**"

I slam the computer closed and rest my head in my hands. "Why?" I say to no one there, the TV emitting muffled sounds in the other room where Al sits, fixated. Not feeling successful in conversations and unable to hear television dialogue well, I'm avoiding both lately—even with my husband. I feel like I'm drifting away from Al, from life, from myself.

1970

I am five years old, riding home on the bus from my first week of kindergarten in Poway, California. When the bus pulls to the stop at the end of our housing development, a short walk from our house, I look out the window for my mother. She is there waiting for me, and I'm so excited to see her. I walk down the aisle to the front of the bus and begin to step down the stairs when I feel a hand land hard on my shoulder. I turn to face the driver, a round lady with short curly hair.

"Michele, this is not your stop. You aren't getting off here."

I'm confused. I know it is my stop. I boarded here earlier this morning, and I can see my mother right out the window.

"This is my stop. And my mom is right over there," I say, pointing behind the bus.

"No. Your tag right here says your stop is the next one—Rancho Bernardo," she double taps the square sticker on my chest. "Sit back down."

I move back and turn around, searching for my mom's eyes out the row of windows. I want her to notice me so I can get her attention. I want her to come and tell the driver this is my stop.

"Michele, I said sit down."

I sit and stare out the big square window just as the door of the bus closes and the engine revs. As we move forward, I think my mom sees me, but she doesn't wave or react at all. I watch her turn her back and calmly walk away back toward home. I don't understand. As the sight of her short jet-black hair fades in the distance, I begin to quietly cry.

As the bus continues on, I sit in my seat, wondering what will happen. I don't recognize any of the surroundings. When the bus stops again, I watch a couple of older kids get up and off. The driver calls my name while looking at me through the big mirror above her round steering wheel. She tells me to come forward. I walk slowly up the aisle.

"Rancho Bernardo," she taps my tag with her index finger, "this is your stop."

"But it's not," I say, shaking my head as tears drop from the corner of my eyes and fall to the floor.

"I am sure it is. Let's go look."

She points down the stairs and out the open door. I step across to the sidewalk, and she follows. We both look around. Nothing looks familiar to me, and my mother is not there. I glance over at oncoming cars, hoping each one that approaches is my mom's blue Chevy Impala. None of them are. None of them stop. I want to tell this lady again that my mom was at the last stop and now she's gone, but I don't. I can't find my voice. After several more excruciating seconds, the driver lets out an exasperated sigh.

"Let's get back on the bus."

The drive feels especially long as I watch all the other kids arrive at their stops, many whose mothers are there to greet them with big smiles and bear hugs. We've stopped probably six more times and then I'm the only one left on the bus. I keep thinking terrible thoughts. What if I never see my mom again? What if she's decided she doesn't want me anymore? Am I purposely being sent somewhere else? Why isn't she trying to find me?

The ride ends at the place it began—school. The bus driver walks with me to the front office, and as she opens the door, the only person inside is the secretary. While the two converse, I stand feeling nervous and afraid until the secretary walks around the high counter, takes my hand, and leads me to a row of chairs off to the right.

"We will call your mother, okay?"

I nod and try to stop my quivering lip.

What feels like hours later, the door swings open. It's my mother. I run to her, press my face against her hips, and hold on tight.

CHAPTER 9

JULY 1998

After reading *Goodnight Moon* to the boys and cleaning up the kitchen, I plop down next to Al on the couch as he watches the last minutes of a Seinfeld episode. I ask him to turn up the volume so I can hear it better, but I'm sure it's already loud to him. I don't like watching television much anymore. It's become the same as listening to music. There's a distortion present, and sometimes, all I hear is annoying mumbles. The feeling of ease and relaxation at these times has been replaced with irritation and stress. As I sit staring at the images on the screen, I wonder if hearing aids will help or if they'll be like that amplifier— picking up too many sounds at once. At the commercial break, Al asks me what I'm thinking about.

"That you and I have been married for eight years, I'm only thirty two years old, and I already need hearing aids. It scares me. I want to grow old with you, but not this fast."

"It will be okay."

"I want to get them because I know I'm not functioning very well, but I don't want to get them because I'm mad I have to. That it's come to this."

"Get the best possible ones out there."

"But they're expensive, Al. Digital ones can run about four thousand dollars, and Kaiser won't cover them."

"That's all right. They're going to be like new ears for you. Can't put a price on that."

I nod and sigh, then smile, "True. Thanks, honey."

I'm pleasantly surprised by Al's reaction because he's always been money conscious and tightfisted. His kindness and support make me feel less alone. I scoot closer on the couch to him and while leaning my head on his shoulder, think about finding good hearing aids that are small and unnoticeable. I wonder what hearing aids in my ears will feel like and start dreaming about how great it will be to hear again.

Walking into Sierra Hearing Services, I assume there will be elderly people sitting in the waiting room. I'm wrong. There's a child about five years old and the same size as Brennan moving toward the exit, holding his mother's hand. Both of his ears hold thick cream-colored hearing aids with clear tubes circling the outside. I hold open the door, smile, and offer a warm hello. I reflect on the loneliness I've been feeling lately and wonder, is it like he has new ears?

As I face the young receptionist wearing a friendly smile, she offers a well-enunciated, "Good morning. How are you today?" that's comforting and audible to me. I tell her I'm doing fine, give her my name, and let her know I have an appointment with Laurinda Mattson before taking my seat in the empty waiting area. My eyes scan the walls of nature scenes and advertisements for various types of hearing aids featuring quotes like "So you can hear what you've been missing."

An attractive woman with stylish short blond hair and a feminine yet athletic build walks over to greet me. She extends her hand and says in a friendly tone, "I'm Laurinda."

I'm guessing she's about forty-five, and as I look into her blue eyes, I see warmth and like her immediately. I follow her to a private room and hand her the audiology reports I've brought with me. She crinkles her eyes as she reviews them and asks me what my doctors have said. I share the history of the past months and the diagnosis.

After responding with compassion about all the unknowns, she says, "Let's work on aiding both ears." She explains that while there hasn't been much hearing ability in my left ear since childhood, we can tap into what exists to help that ear too. She takes an ear mould impression, placing small soft, egg-shaped pieces inside both ears. While explaining the benefits of digital hearing aids and how they can be custom programmed to my hearing ability, she enunciates with intention and looks directly at me while she speaks. I follow every word with ease. She's the first person in months I feel as though I can understand well and who understands my situation. I'm gaining hope. In two weeks, the aids will be ready. Laurinda says then, I will have the assistance I need in order to hear again.

I'm sitting with Laurinda again in mid-July, during my monthlong summer break from work.

"Your aids arrived, and I've already programmed them, but we may need to make some minor adjustments."

I watch her hook each custom-shaped device up to a computer, check the program on the screen, nod, disconnect them, and move toward me. They aren't bulky and big. I'm relieved.

"I'll place them in your ears and adjust the fit. It could take a few weeks, maybe even a month, to get used to having something sitting in your ears, okay? You can start by wearing them for a few hours at a time."

"Okay," I nod, feeling a bit anxious. I'm unsure what this is going to be like as she places them in my ears as far as they can go.

"Ready?" she stands back by the computer, and I nod before answering.

"Yes," I say and am startled.

"How is that? To hear your own voice?"

"Oh my gosh. I hear my own voice, and I hear yours! Well!" My face lights up. "I can hear out of my left ear now too. I-I can't remember ever being able to."

"I'm going to keep talking for a little while so you can see how things sound as I back up and move closer, and I'm going to add in some other noises too."

While she makes conversation, I hear her every word, and I smile. When she picks up papers and opens her desk drawer, I can hear them—sounds I know I wouldn't have heard earlier. I can't tell where some of the other sounds are coming from, but I do hear them. I feel like I've been given an injection of life. Laurinda asks me how I'm doing..

"I...it's great. I can hear things I couldn't hear for sure." My eyes get watery. This time, with joy.

"One-on-one conversations will still be the easiest," she adds. "There may be some overwhelm in noisier environments. I want us to take a walk outside so you can hear what it's like out there too.

I suggest you give yourself some time to adjust to varying sounds and situations."

As we stand up and move toward the door, a cacophony of sounds hits my ears, things I haven't heard for five months now. The little squeak as the door opens, my footsteps on the linoleum hallway floor, the receptionist's voice from afar. When we open the front door and step outside, it's as if the volume rises. I hear car doors closing, voices, heels on the sidewalk, even some birds, but they sound somewhat different than they used to. No longer muffled or fuzzy, just different. I'm trying to find the words to explain it when I notice a very strange loud noise unfamiliar to me. I turn to Laurinda.

"What's that?" My eyes scan the area, and my brain feels like it's trying to decipher it.

"It's the garbage truck behind the building picking up dumpsters." She watches my reaction.

"Oh." I pause and listen longer.

The garbage truck doesn't sound the same to me as it did before I lost my hearing. She notices.

"There will be some sounds you have to readjust to," she explains. "Your brain will retrain itself to associate some of the newer sounds as you identify them."

"Why is sound different now though?"

"Because hearing aids don't restore normal hearing. They never will. But they get as close as possible."

When we walk back inside, I realize there will be a learning curve. I think I expected sound to be like it was originally. It's not. I watch Laurinda teach me how to change the small round batteries, opening the delicate compartment door on the outside of each aid. I learn about the cleaning tool to use to remove little remnants of earwax near the microphone hole, and how to be careful to not stick the wand inside too far. I find out about a high-pitched squeal the aids make if someone comes up and covers my ears with their hands, or even if a hat sits too close. A feedback of sorts that is very unpleasant. Laurinda cautions me to take them out before showering or jumping in a swimming pool. And at night, they will need to be removed for sleeping.

Before I can think about it, I reach out and hug Laurinda.

Driving home, I notice the rhythmic clicking of the turn signal I've forgotten about. I wonder if I'll be able to hear whispers, my cat Midnight's meow, or a knock at the door. I'm surging with hope and excited to rediscover all the sounds I had forgotten I was missing.

CHAPTER 10

OCTOBER 1998

As the next days and months pass, I practice life wearing hearing aids. At first, they get itchy and irritating after a few hours; but over time, this goes away, just like Laurinda said. I'm relaxed and able to communicate much better during one-to-one conversations. I still tend to look at people's mouths as they speak. Learning to lip-read—carefully watching the movement of the mouth while words are spoken, matching form with sound—is still a great strategy for me.

Big group discussions, such as meetings at work, are still challenging. With lots of people talking, I have trouble determining where voices are coming from and identifying who is speaking. I scan the room, searching in what feels like slow motion to detect the source of what I hear, with curious eyes watching and waiting for me to respond. My skin starts feeling clammy as I feel the pressure to be accurate. Often, I guess the direction of the voice only to find that it originates from the opposite side. Doctors say this is something that hearing aids cannot help me with. I have up days and down days. Many scenarios continue to be challenging. I didn't expect that the telephone would emit terrible squeals of feedback during phone conversations. I can't seem to adjust to the loud volume in movie theaters; and rooms with poor acoustics, foreign accents, and ambient noises leave me at a loss.

I stand before the bathroom mirror, adding finishing sweeps of mascara for work. I bring my hands up behind my head to grab my hair and pull it back into a ponytail, just to look. While the hearing aids fit snugly inside the canals of my ears and don't have any tubes trailing behind, I can still see them and their beige color. I'm still feeling self-conscious and embarrassed about them, even though I'm thankful they help me hear. I don't think I am ready to have them in plain sight. I don't want to deal with the questions I assume will follow: *What are those? Why do you have them?* Or better yet, *What happened? Why can't you hear?* I release my bunched hand and allow the strands of hair to fall back on each side of my face. I smooth the locks and pull them closer to my cheeks, making sure nothing is noticeable. I don't want people to know I'm hearing impaired.

I'm still hoping that wearing hearing aids will be temporary and that doctors will find out why my hearing left and fix it. I'm happy that I'm hearing better with assistance, but hearing aids can only tap into the hearing ability I do have. They aren't true sound. It's not like putting on a pair of eyeglasses. There is no twenty-twenty adjusted hearing, I've learned. I want to be young and vibrant like I should be after just turning thirty-three. I want to wear my hair in a ponytail without feeling deeply flawed, as if I don't belong with everybody else.

1976

I walk out the door of my classroom at recess and head across the blacktop past the chants of long-rope jumpers toward Kristen, Samantha, and Patrice, three girls from the other fifth grade classroom next door. I've been playing and having fun with them at school for months, and it's our regular plan to meet up at recess.

On this day though, Paula Edwards, who's in my class and happens to be the most popular girl in our grade, stands beside my friends. With hands on her hips, Paula tosses her short hair from side to side as if it were long. I greet them all when I approach and ask to join in. Paula looks me up and down, and shoots an expression of disapproval. I sense hostility, and my skin starts to sting. Paula turns away, cups a hand around her mouth filled with new braces, and pulls Kristen in closer. She whispers something in her ear. I have no idea what she says, but both of them look at me and laugh out loud. Paula holds her smile of mockery longer than Kristen while using her whole hand to signal them all into a private huddle of four. In between rustles of breath and snide sneers, Paula points right at me. Her finger looks especially long as she holds it out. The giggles get louder and louder, and she is the conductor. I don't understand. What have I done to deserve this?

I turn and swallow, taking my first steps away without saying anything. I hear louder footsteps approach before strands of my long curly light-brown hair are pulled hard from the back of my head. I turn back around to more laughter and Paula rolling her eyes.

"Oh, does that hurt?" she says in a mocking, high-pitched voice, and snickers again to prompt her small audience for back up. I'm about to open my mouth and tell her to stop it when she steps heavily on my toes exposed through my sandals.

"Oh, does that hurt too?"

I feel like the laughter of the girls is going to smother me until Paula shoves me with both hands. I have to steady myself on my heels so I don't fall back. I feel my face burn with unexpressed rage.

"We don't like you," she says. "Go away."

I turn and run. I flee stones of hurt and exile, and run straight into a cold loneliness that immediately envelopes me. I run all the way to the edge of school grounds and see cars along Santa Anita Avenue. My plan is to keep going until I reach home. But soon, I am intercepted by Mrs. Bowen, the school counselor. She emerges from the office and calls out my name. I stop and surrender, and she comes to my side, leading me back to her office where she offers me a box of Kleenex. I tell her what happened and that I want to go home and never come back. That I don't understand how Paula can be so popular when she is so mean. That she seems to possess some type of unspoken spell over others.

"I don't have any friends anymore, and everyone wants Paula to be their friend." I snivel and wipe my nose.

"Or maybe she's the girl nobody wants as their enemy," Mrs. Bowen says as she leans toward me and pats my knee. "You're not her first victim, and you won't be her last."

Mrs. Bowen might be right. But my ten-year-old self only believes that something must be terribly wrong with me if Paula and my friends turned against me so quickly.

CHAPTER 11

NOVEMBER 1998

I hate it when Al has to tap me on the shoulder to get my attention in the middle of the night, when my hearing aids are tucked away safely in my nightstand. It's happening more than weekly these days.

"Hey, hey," he shakes my arm next and speaks louder. "Wake up!"

Startled from deep sleep, I open my eyes and sit up fast. "What? What's wrong?"

"Brennan is calling you!"

I fling the bedcovers off me and start to run around the bed toward the hallway, not hearing one iota of a sound, when I remember that I don't have my hearing aids in. I return to my nightstand, open the black box, and put them in as fast as I can.

"I'm coming, sweetie," I listen to myself announce with confident reassurance and get to him as soon as I can.

I don't want to be the type of mother that doesn't come when her four-year-old or one-year-old needs her. I want to be there for the bad dream, the achy tooth, the sudden stomach pain, or the moments when darkness and shadows get too scary.

Having to take out my hearing aids every night before I go to sleep feels like a jolt of instant silence and isolation. A harsh reminder of my vulnerability and deafness, and the temporary nature of these cream-colored devices I rely on to help me function.

Brennan and I are in his room putting toys away. Perhaps due to noise of toys being tossed in the toy box while he talks, I can't decipher the words he's saying.

"What did you say, sweetie?"

He pauses for a moment and begins to speak. I watch his lips, but I can't make out his collection of vocalized sounds when he turns his back mid-sentence.

"Brennan, I…I'm sorry. Can you say it one more time for me?" I wince, concentrate harder, and focus with determination. I hear two distinct words this time.

"Never mind," he says with emphasis on "mind," his gaze shifting downward. These two little words spoken by a four-year-old sear beyond measure. I watch him shake his head, like he's shaking off annoyance in slow motion.

"I'm…I'm sorry, sweetie. I…please say it one more time," I plead, as I sit down where he stands to get closer to his level.

"Never mind," he says clear and loud.

I know these words are not his original message. I open my

mouth to respond but stop when I notice his steps of defeat as he turns and walks away. I feel defeat too.

The words replay over and over in my head. *Never mind. Never mind.* Like it doesn't matter anyway. *Like maybe I don't matter anyway.* His words feel like punishment and get amplified in my head. *No more chances. You already missed it twice, and it was twice too much. So never damn mind.*

I sit there in silent loneliness despite wearing aids, still wishing for the ability to hear. Really hear. This sentence of silence and the solitary confinement that accompanies it is sometimes too hard to handle. Yet I can't do a damn thing about it.

Later, when I tuck Brennan into bed and finish reading him a story, I tell him that sometimes I hear better than others. It pains me that at age four, he's being asked to understand something I don't understand either. I remind him that early in the morning or late at night, it is harder for me to hear him because I have to take out my hearing aids. I maintain a positive tone though, and remind him that he can come into Mommy and Daddy's room and tap me to wake me up if I ever don't respond to his voice.

"I always want you to be able to come to me if you need me and I don't hear you calling out, okay?"

"Okay, Mommy," he says solemnly like a grown up, nodding his head.

"I'm sorry I didn't hear you very well today. You're important to me, and what you say is important to me."

"That's okay."

"Well, it's not okay with me, but I'm doing the best I can. I love you, Brennan."

"I love you too!" He throws arms around my neck, and I sink into this feeling of unconditional love.

CHAPTER 12

2014

Today feels like we are truly in Antarctica. Everything is extreme: the white, wind, waves, and bone-chilling temperatures. Naturalists on the ship have planned a passenger excursion to nearby Weinke Island, a place of glaciers, snow, and ice, inhabited only by a colony of Gentoo penguins.

I feel the push of freezing air when it's my turn to step out the ship's doorway toward the portable metal staircase. A Zodiac waits two levels below, and six bundled-up people, only their noses visible, have already boarded for our excursion. With a guide on each side of me, I'm instructed to hold onto the handrails and climb carefully down. Gloves cover my hands, but because they are so thick, I don't feel a solid grasp of these metal posts. I concentrate on taking slow, careful steps. At the bottom, two other guides assist my entrance into the sturdy rubber boat. After I sit down, I see Gordon enter and sit beside me. He pats my knee and smiles with his eyes. After two final passengers step across us, our guide boards, stands at the back, and pulls the Zodiac away from the ship.

I concentrate on the only sounds—the engine, harsh howls of wind, sloshing sea, and crackles of ice—as we move through waves of whitecaps. We travel through sea ice chunks as if inside a blender, but when larger icebergs appear, our guide maneuvers to avoid them. I lean my body toward the center of the boat as splashes and sprays hit the back and side of my waterproof jacket. Sometimes, I squeeze my eyes shut.

I fear falling in this freezing Southern ocean of turbulence. I wonder how long I would last if I went in. With wind in my face and shaking legs, I open my eyes to see one guy holding up a GoPro. As we pull closer, I see hundreds of identical black and white dressed creatures assembled closely in groups, all of them about three feet high. Unaffected by our approach, they exude charisma and cuteness right away. My nervousness shifts to excitement.

One by one, we are instructed to scoot our bottoms up along the rubber boat's edge to the front. I turn around by lifting my legs up and outside the boat, and reach for the guide's outstretched hand. I stand up on large dark rocks submerged in the ocean below my boots while powerful gusts continue. My legs quiver while the waves push against my knees. The winds make it hard to hear the guide's directive shout, "Move forward, walk across the jagged black rocks, and climb up there." She points at an ice shelf. It takes all my effort to climb out of the water onto the lip of thick ice in my GORE-TEX waterproof pants. When I stand up, I notice two things: my wobbly legs and my wet gloves.

Gordon puts his arms around me and holds me for a moment, sensing my anxiety. Next, I remove my no-longer-absorbent gloves. I immediately notice the red of my hands and rub my palms together. Fortunately, I have a second pair of gloves in my jacket pocket. While I reach for them with my right hand, and feel myself shiver, a guide grabs my cold left hand and places it between her gloved hands to warm. I'm breathing faster. My heart is racing, and I worry it's taking way too long for me to get them on. I feel like the lone novice, suddenly homesick for comforting conditions. When dry gloves are on, I take a deep breath of gratitude for the little gesture of preparedness and Gordon's calming presence beside me.

Glancing left, I see more black and white creatures with their prominent bright orange beaks. Hundreds of them. Some waddle, their wings outstretched, while others snooze on their bellies in the snow or stand in groups. I walk closer and watch with intent curiosity. I kneel down gently on the ice. I take some photographs and study their movements. They exhibit no fear or concern of human visitors and don't attempt to avoid us. Their thick webbed feet are a lighter shade of orange than their beaks. Watching these small penguins walk with their precious side-to-side shuffle, their fanned out black tassels of tails moving too, makes me giggle. Their missteps, trips, and hops are awkward and adorable like a puppy finding its footing. With a sudden gust of icy, gritty wind, some of the penguins blow right over. They seem totally unfazed and completely comfortable picking themselves right back up. They aren't concerned about the cold or the harsh conditions of this white continent. I watch them and take lessons from their cheerful resilience.

A unique aroma permeates the air, and I realize it's coming from the pinkish-brown stains on the white ice called Guano, a fancy name for penguin poop. While it isn't pleasant, it's not offensive either. Just distinct. It's the only smell I notice while we're in Antarctica.

I hear the calls and cackles of the penguins and wonder what they're communicating about. I recall some facts shared by one of the naturalists about these penguins and their means of identification. They rely heavily on hearing and conveying sound, more so than vision. I contemplate the importance of this sense. The critical life aspect of it.

CHAPTER 13

MARCH 1999

"Let's take a Sunday drive in the Vette. I want to show you something," Al announces with a hint of mystery after his mom picks up the boys for an afternoon visit. We hop in the 1962 white Corvette convertible, one of his favorite toys born the same year as him. This car was Al's first major purchase after we both graduated from Chico State. It is also the vehicle in which we cruised the oceanfront streets of Pacific Grove and Monterey on the weekend in 1989 when he asked me to marry him. As we drive down tree-lined streets out of our neighborhood, I'm transported back to that time.

The engine's purr along the two-lane Ocean Drive blends in with the sound of rolling waves and surf slapping the sand. We travel slowly while my elbow rests on the passenger door, the convertible top down, the smell of seaweed lingering in the springtime air. It was Al's idea to come to Monterey for the weekend, and his plans include a coastal picnic. He's stopped along the side of the road twice already to get out and look for the right spot, but then continued farther along the scenic highway. The sky is a vibrant blue decorated with wisps of thin clouds. The sun on my skin feels nourishing without being intense, and with our sunglasses on, we smile at each other, taking in the vast views.

Slowly, Al pulls off onto the gravelly shoulder.

"Wait here. Let me see if this is a good place." He opens his door and gets out fast. I turn my head and watch him walk behind the car and down a sandy embankment. He returns quickly. "Yep. This is perfect. I'm going to set it all up, okay, while you stay here. Then I will come back and get you." He takes a picnic basket out of the trunk of the car, flashes a proud smile, and heads down again beneath the roadside, hidden from my view.

While I sit, I wonder about what Al is up to with this picnic. This particular day does not hold specific significance to us, but we have been dating for five years, been out of college for two, and both have solid jobs—me as a teacher and he as a systems engineer. I wonder for a moment if he is going to propose, knowing how much I love the ocean. It's taking him a little while to set up the picnic, and I tell myself if this is "that" day, I would probably notice immediately.

Al appears from the sand. When I get out of the Corvette, he takes my hand and leads me down from the road and across some rugged rocks to an open area of golden sand where a red and white striped picnic blanket is spread out in a giant square. A bottle of champagne and two glasses sit center stage, and two plastic plates with cutlery are placed across from each other. I smile at him when I see the arrangement, and he smiles back before leading us to sit on the blanket and open the bubbles.

I'm a combination of nerves and excitement. Our years as boyfriend-girlfriend have been stormy. Many of my friends have asked, "Is he affectionate, loving, and attentive enough?" While truthfully he's not much of the time, I feel as though he shows me glimpses of a softer side. A side he rarely displays to anyone else. I'm thinking maybe I could be the one to bring those warm-hearted, more caring characteristics to the surface. My thoughts these past months have been repetitive: *I want to be married, want to have children. What if this is as good as it gets? What if this is the guy that's out there for me and there isn't anyone else? Wouldn't I rather have the roller-coaster relationship than be alone?*

For a little while on the beach, we just talk and sit and sip, and comment on the beautiful weather and scenery. There's no hurriedness and no leading conversation about "us." When I ask what is on the lunch menu, Al opens the basket and tips it to show me a variety of fruits, deli meats, and cheese. Then he says he has an idea before we eat.

"Let's build a sandcastle!" He crawls into the sand and makes a large perimeter circle that extends close to me. "This will be the moat," he says and tosses me a plastic bucket.

I watch him begin shoveling with his own little bucket and follow on my side. About three scoops later, my bucket hits something beneath the sand. I dig a bit deeper and put the bucket aside. A square piece of something with a white strap on it comes into view. I brush off the sand to take a closer look at it.

"Something is buried here in the sand. Like a kid's toy or something."

"What is it?"

"I don't know."

I'm curious enough to keep moving sand off and away from it, and in my mind, I'm conjuring up the story that some little kid must've left a sand toy here. I wonder if it's been lost or deliberately left and for how long.

The more sand I clear off, the more I can see the white strap. I place my fingers underneath it and pull up. Slowly, a square box appears from beneath. A box with a handle and a bunch of Mickey Mouse designs decorating all four sides. I lift it up to examine it more closely and say aloud, "It's a Jack in the Box." Al leans over, brushes the top and side of it too, and offers a semi-interested, "Hmm."

I turn the handle on the right side and hear the familiar tune of "Pop Goes the Weasel."

I continue and expect that the top is going to open at any moment, but it doesn't. Al leans over and brushes more sand out of the grooves of the top while I wonder if it's a broken toy that was discarded. He suggests I try again. I turn the handle, and all of a sudden, the top flies open. Mickey Mouse sways side to side, holding a sign in his hands that says: "Will You Marry Me?" On Mickey's head is a hat that has been made from a ring box. A beautiful diamond in a band of gold gleams in the sunshine.

I read the words again because I am stunned and confused, and then I look with wide eyes at Al who has tears in his. And then I realize, he has planned all of this. This *is* his proposal, and the softer side of him is on full display in this moment. I shake my head in amazed joy, take the ring off Mickey's head, and look right at Al.

"Yes," I say while I put the band on my ring finger. "Yes yes yes!"

I'm pulled back to the present moment as Al starts telling me he has a surprise. Al is good at surprises. He knows I love them. Still a man of few feeling-type words, he prefers to display affection with action rather than touch or terms of endearment. At times like these, it's okay with me.

I wonder if he's trying to cheer me up. I've been constantly irritable and noticeably annoyed at how difficult it still is to participate in conversation even wearing hearing aids. Is he feeling sorry for me? Is he aware of how much I've been struggling this past year?

I feel a refreshing sense of joy and freedom as my long hair whips and tickles my cheek, even though the sound of the wind feels foreign. We drive out of town, heading east before we exit the freeway into territory resembling boondocks. I have no idea where we are.

We cruise through an established residential neighborhood, and I watch the street signs change from Marina View to Lake Crest to Outrigger Drive as we climb a hill. The purr of the engine enhances the ascent, setting the stage for the summit. My eyes grow to the size of golf balls, and I release an immediate, "Oh wow!" at the incredible, unobstructed view. Calm blue waters of the vast Folsom Lake provide a glorious backdrop, while in front of us are twenty-one fresh homesite lots for sale. All of them feature waterfront views.

We pull up alongside the parcel directly in front of us. Al turns off the key and steps out of the car. I stare at open landscape, mature oak trees, and soaring ospreys.

"Oh my gosh, it's beautiful here. How did you find this?" I glance around in amazement. We've both dreamed of living near the water someday.

"I took a drive yesterday looking for avenues leading to the lake. I stumbled across this and said the same 'wow' you did. There's even a path down there that leads to the marina." I notice he's making more of a habit of looking at me directly when he speaks even when I'm wearing my hearing aids. It makes it much easier for me. I nod and hold his gaze so he knows I hear him.

"Um, are you thinking…well, can we even afford something like this?" I ask, unsure of what it means to be falling in love with this scenery.

He reaches into the front pocket of his khaki shorts, retrieving a folded up piece of paper with a Coldwell Banker realty logo on it and flashes a proud grin, "Well, I think maybe we can!" He shuffles toward me, eager to share prices and various lot size choices.

It's a month later when the Dom Perignon cork flies off into the sky like a firecracker. While sitting on a frayed picnic blanket covering freshly cleared and graded dirt, we cuddle close, raise our flutes, and toast to our dream home.

"I can design the architectural structure of the house using a computer program. I'll create walls of windows to capture these views." His eyes hold sparkles while he uses his hands as he speaks.

"Sounds great, Al." I take a sip of bubbles and envision living here.

"What do you think about gathering ideas this summer on

interior stuff? You know, paint colors, carpets, flooring, and kitchen appliances? We'll have lots of decisions to make, and I want to be prepared when we select a builder."

"I'd love to. Summer's coming up and it's good timing." We pick up our flutes and clink them together again.

I start feeling like this shared dream will be a saving grace for me, given the fact that it's been over a year since I lost my hearing, and lately, it's been plummeting again. I need something else to concentrate on. A project to beautify. An inspiring creation of newness, happiness, and warmth.

What I haven't told my husband, or anyone else for that matter, is that I have been trying to ignore a creeping feeling within that something's deeply amiss. I'm beginning to wonder if something is seriously wrong with me. Not just physically, but deeper than that. Maybe something is wrong with who I am at my very core.

I decide this brand-new dream house will be the replacement for my stirring discontent. Rich-looking decor, airy high ceilings, walls of windows, healthy stainless steel appliances, the aroma of fresh paint and new carpet. Brand-new beginnings for everything. I wrap myself in the promise of it.

CHAPTER 14

TWO YEARS LATER

February 2001

Another afternoon, stuck in traffic during my monster commute, I restlessly contemplate calling my mother-in-law. Since last August, I've been working full time as a principal in El Dorado Hills in preparation of moving into our new house this spring, but I spend forty-five minutes traveling each way in the meantime. I'm not going to make it by 6:00 p.m. Again. I hate it when this happens. I never pictured myself as the mom rushing from work to pick up the last children at day care. A wonderful back up, she lives close by, and Brennan and Trevor always love seeing her. I keep glancing at my watch as if expecting time to move slower. I reach into my bottomless purse to fish out my cell phone.

"Hi, Maria. It's Michele. I'm crawling along the freeway, and I'm worried I won't make it back in time to pick up the boys. Any chance you can grab them for me?" I wince a bit, not wanting to inconvenience her again. It has happened twice in the past five days.

"All right. I'll pick them up, feed them some dinner, and drop them off in about two hours on my way to church." Her Portuguese accent fills my ear, eliciting a little squeal from my hearing aid as I try to place the phone to my ear without getting feedback and drive at the same time.

"That would be great." My shoulders drop away from my chin. "Thank you so much."

Al is home and already changed from dress slacks into shorts when I walk in the door at 6:10 p.m., an unusual but welcome surprise. Hurrying to get out of my heels and nylons, I am excited to make dinner for just the two of us, a rare occasion. After throwing together a simple chicken and rice casserole with a mushroom soup sauce and putting it in the oven, I pour myself a glass of chardonnay and grab a cold beer out of the fridge for Al as he walks into the kitchen. With more zeal in his voice than his usual weekday small talk about his work as a vice president of sales, Al mentions a consultant named Brett who's been working with his company, doing executive team building.

"He uses personality profile questionnaires and then reviews and compares them, examining various combinations between workers' styles, strengths, and weaknesses." I watch Al's dark-brown eyes brighten when he talks about how communication is opening up within his department due to the process. I listen and nod as Al elaborates, "And Brett pulled me aside today and told me about some training here in Sacramento about leadership, communication, and something he called like, uh, emotional intelligence."

"Interesting. Are you going to go?" I ask eagerly. I'm hoping he's gained interest in expanding his level of sensitivity as I've been hurt by some of the cold-hearted comments he's directed at me lately.

"No no. I, um, told him it wasn't my kind of thing, but it sounded like something you could use and would probably be more interested in doing. He'd be up for telling you more about it if you'd like. I was thinking maybe we could invite him over for dinner anyway, while he's in town." He takes a swig of his Corona.

"Hmm, okay. Sounds kinda interesting."

I wonder why he isn't interested and what makes him think I would be. And then, last Sunday replays in my mind.

It had been late in the afternoon when I noticed it again. The feeling of uneasiness swirling around in my stomach, stealing the fun out of the remaining seven hours of my waking weekend. It had become like clockwork over past months. Every Sunday evening, the mere thought of Monday morning consumed me with dread. My breathing would become rapid as I predicted all the energy it would take for me to get through the week of work with my limited hearing.

I consider that perhaps with this offer, Al is looking out for me. I became an elementary school principal six years ago, at the age of twenty-nine, after four years of teaching and four more as a vice principal. Being a working mom now in charge of over five hundred students and forty-five staff members has been full of unforeseen challenges interspersed with a little prestige and many meaningful moments. While I am good at my job, I don't always

THIS KIND OF SILENCE

think it's good for me. I give so much of myself in hope that I can benefit hundreds of children, yet don't get to spend enough time to feel effective with the two of my own. I need better balance. Perhaps I should look more into this "emotional intelligence" training. Maybe it would at least help ease my Sunday-night blues.

Two nights later, Al greets Brett at the front door. Tall, with an air of charisma and a seventies-like swagger, Brett walks toward me and introduces himself with friendliness and warmth. During dinner, I watch Al and Brett throw back a swig of beer at the same time after Brett uses sports analogies to explain coaching employees in the workplace. Brett radiates a presence that takes up a lot of space in the room. He speaks every word with volume, authority, and conviction. He's a skilled conversationalist and passionate about his career.

Midway through the evening, in between bites, Brett enthusiastically shares his experience attending a training called NLI, short for Next Level Intensive. He explains that the overriding theme is leadership.

"Knowing myself as a leader helps me be a better leader in the workplace," he says. He tells us that the workshop is divided into two sessions—a three-day session over a weekend followed by a five-day residential session requiring a hotel stay two weeks later. Al listens casually but fidgets often in his chair and excuses himself, leaving Brett and me together at the table.

Brett leans over and speaks with kindness, "Al tells me you have been having some health issues too, Michele. That you're having problems with your hearing and that doctors aren't finding any medical reason for it."

I nod slowly, looking at his sapphire-blue eyes intently.

"I can't help but wonder if there is some emotional component involved as well. For example, a respected author named Louise Hay would say, 'What is it you are afraid to hear or don't want to hear?'" He raises his eyes to expose lines on his forehead and holds the expression. I wonder what exactly Al has told him about me.

His eye contact is uncomfortably intense.

"Uh, what? What was that again?"

"Louise Hay. She would ask, 'What is it you maybe don't want to hear?'"

His words linger in the kitchen air, and his eyes seek a reaction from me. I feel annoyance about what he is suggesting. A rush of defensiveness ignites in my chest. *Is he saying I don't want to hear? Is he suggesting that I am causing my hearing issues? Who the hell is Louise Hay anyway? What does he mean "What is it I don't want to hear?" Of course, I want to hear.* My heart beats fast and I want to say something. No words come out. I sit with Brett in awkward silence, my eyes darting around as my brain attempts to make some kind of sense of this suggestion.

"Who? Um, who is Louise?" I say awkwardly, desperately hiding my irritation.

"Louise Hay. She's an author of a book called *Heal Your Life*. I thought, well, maybe it could help."

I see compassion in Brett's face and a quiet voice within me says I cannot simply dismiss his questions.

When he leaves, Brett gives me the name and number of the psychologist, Dr. Wu, who leads the NLI training and encourages me to call and get more information.

"That workshop changed my life, Michele," he says before

turning and walking to his rental car in the driveway. "I'm excited for you!" He rests both hands on his hips, pauses, and flashes a big smile.

I reflect on Brett's words over the next five days at work and most seriously after an angry parent stomps through the front office door and demands that I fix the parking lot congestion so she can drop off her daughter and not be late to work every day. I consider the workshop again after a father scolds me for not making his son miss his recesses when he doesn't eat all the contents of his sack lunch. Unsure if better communication skills are the answer, I do know I need confidence, calmness, and clarity to more effectively cope with conflict; so I decide I will call Dr. Wu.

At home, I sit on my bed and pick up the phone. I introduce myself to Dr. Wu, tell him about my work, and share that I've spoken with Brett Miles recently. I notice his low-tone voice immediately, so I turn up the handset volume and hold it away from my ear to prevent feedback.

"So you're interested in greater confidence, conflict resolution, and higher self-esteem?

"Yes. And handling stress better and being happier, you know, with work and juggling it all."

"Well, leadership skills soar when you learn who you are as a leader first. Your results are long lasting because we get to the origin of your issues."

When I hang up fifteen minutes later, I'm feeling pangs of hope and excitement.

After reading the boys both a Dr. Seuss story before bed, I find Al sitting on the black leather couch watching Seinfeld. I plop myself down beside him.

"Hey, I'm really glad you told me about this training, Al. I think it would help me a lot especially with conflict and dealing with difficult people. I've found out more, and I really want to go."

"How much is it?" he asks immediately, his dark-brown eyes still fixed on the TV.

I'm hesitant to reply. It is a lot of money. "Well, um, it's pretty expensive. But it includes a hotel stay for four nights and eight all-day training sessions. It's, uh, twenty-two hundred and ninety dollars."

"That's too much," he replies quickly and matter-of-factly, shaking his head no.

"Uh, yeah, it is a lot, I know. I actually asked Brett about that. He said he totally understands the concern, but it's worth every penny and that I will know that afterward. I have a good feeling about it for some reason, Al. Please. I would really like to do this."

He snickers a bit before responding, "We are building a house, Michele. A huge house full of everything you want. I don't think we can afford that right now. It's bad timing." He still doesn't look at me.

I drop the conversation, feeling like a bright balloon with a pinhole leak. We sit in silence, and nothing more is said. I can't help but think about why Al would bring up the training idea and invite Brett over if he thinks it is too expensive. Didn't he ask Brett about that?

In bed later, my mind chatter plays relentlessly. While I know it is true that building our dream house is a significant investment and the training is expensive, I don't understand why Al's response was just "no," when it was his suggestion in the first place. Why do I feel as though what he says goes and I have no say in it? I toss and turn restlessly, unable to sleep.

1974

Inside our home on this rainy Saturday afternoon, my brother Mark and I play Buds, a game we imagined up together. Mark's character is Pat Knox. Mine is Chris Clark. Both are colleagues of Dad's at the insurance company where he works. We act out silly scenes pretending to be these men while we each wear one of Dad's ties hanging around our neck.

"Hi, Bud," I say with a deep male-sounding voice.

"Hi, Bud," he copies me, his voice even deeper.

The attempt to act and talk like grown-ups sends us into a fit of giggles. We travel through all the rooms, holding pretend steering wheels between our hands. Drives on the busy freeways of Los Angeles mean horn honks and brakes screeching. We eventually stop at an office and make phone calls to businessmen. We reenact a recent episode from the *Rockford Files*, one of the few television shows we're allowed to watch, and add a car-chase scene. Now we're cracking up after a crash at the bottom of the stairs. Anything one says evokes double laughter from the other. When we add facial expressions, we can't stop the squeals. Our stomachs and cheeks hurt.

Dad enters from the family room without either of us seeing him and stands directly over us. His brows merge with a large wrinkle and his finger points straight up at the ceiling.

"Stop. Stop it! Holy cats! Too much noise! Your mother has a headache. She's laying down up there. Be *quiet!*"

I watch how the lines on Dad's forehead stay raised while he stares at us. *Why is he so mad?*

"We weren't fighting, Dad. We were playing. I...I don't get what the big deal is."

"*She*," he puts his finger in front of my eyes and points up again, "Isn't. Feeling. Well. End of discussion."

I want to tell him that she's never feeling well. That I'm sick of it. But I squelch the words. Instead, I walk past my Dad and rush up the stairs, stomping my feet past her double doors of darkness. When I reach my bedroom door, I grab the edge of it and slam it as hard as I can.

His fiery steps sound five times louder. He flings my door open like a turn of the newspaper and comes at me purple faced with his teeth clenched. He grabs me by my pants, turns me around to lay me over his knee, and pulls my pants and panties down to expose my buttocks, hip, and top of my thigh. I squirm to get away and plead with him loudly.

"No no no. I'm...I'm sorry!"

Whack.

As if it wasn't hard enough, he gives me another.

With no words, he pushes me off, walks past me where I'm crumpled in a heap of sobs, and closes the door behind him. Through salt water and snot, I glance down at the side and back of my thigh. The red tattoos of his handprints sting and throb. I pull my pants gently over them.

When I open my door an hour later, eerie quiet prevails. I walk with caution past Mom's still-closed doors and down the stairs toward the kitchen for some water. Dad sits in his recliner next to the stereo wearing large black headphones. He doesn't acknowledge me when I walk by. I must redeem myself before he will speak to me again. I know this routine. I realize my long-term consequence isn't the red soreness on my skin. It's the lonely banishment of his silent treatment.

CHAPTER 15

MARCH 2001

I'm sitting at a coffee shop with my mom. As I take a sip of my hot, non-fat latte, she asks me how I am.

"I've been feeling this kind of hormonal flight-or-fight response a lot lately, and I think it's anxiety. At first, it was just on Sundays, but it's happening more. And then this guy who's been working with Al's company asked me something I can't get out of my mind, like what I don't want to hear. He said some lady named Louise Hay wrote a book I should read and then he told me about some training here in Sacramento."

"Oh, I know who Louise Hay is. Her book is called *Heal Your Body*. I read it years ago. I think she wrote it in the seventies, actually. It probably would be good to look at it."

"But what is it that I don't want to hear? I don't understand what that even means. It sounds like he thinks I want to be deaf and that's not true."

"Nooo. I think Louise Hay's message is about the importance of loving yourself and using positive affirmations for healing. Is there a Louise Hay training?"

"No. The training is called Next Level Intensive, and the guy who told me about Louise Hay says he took it and it changed his life." I spew out a bunch of details and mention that Dr. Wu, the psychologist who devised the program, indicated that he thought I could benefit from it.

"Wow. Sounds good. When are you going to do it?" Mom's proper English inflection still makes me smile even though she's had it my entire life.

"Well, that's the problem. Al thinks it's too expensive, and it *is* a lot of money. So honestly, I don't think it's going to happen anytime soon."

"Well, it sounds to me like it's very important to you. How much is it?"

I purse my lips together and pause. "It's twenty-two hundred and ninety dollars." I glance over at the boys eating the remains of a chocolate-chip cookie, and I'm waiting for her to tell me that I should just focus on the new house for a while.

"I think you should do it," she says, her teeth showing as she smiles. "I will pay for half of it, and whenever you can pay me back will be fine." She reaches into her black purse, pulls out her navy-blue checkbook, and begins writing me a check. I watch her form the letters for one thousand one hundred forty-five dollars meticulously, noticing the same perfect handwriting I'd admired all my life. I am stunned. She passes it to me, and I get a whiff of her Estee Lauder perfume. "You go do it, Michele. It will be good for you."

1981

I'm placing silverware around a dinner table for two tonight: my boyfriend and me. I'm a sophomore, and it's the Sadie Hawkins Dance, meaning girl gets to invite and treat boy.

"No other couples will be here tonight, right? Just you and Todd." Dad's deep voice is emphatic. This is the condition I must agree to before he and Mom go to the movie theater and leave me with the house.

"Yes." I add a convincing nod and wave them out the door.

While the aroma of baked chicken, rice, and vegetables fill the kitchen, I grin at the bottle of Martinelli's Sparkling Cider my mom placed on the top shelf of the refrigerator with two crystal wine glasses. I use the thirty minutes before Todd arrives to put on my dress, apply some more eye shadow, blush, and mascara, and add a generous helping of hairspray. Todd knocks at the door twenty minutes later wearing charcoal slacks, a gray shirt, and a blue and pink hued tie. After complimenting my dress and learning my parents have left, Todd carries in a large blue ice chest. He sets it down on the living room carpet and opens the lid to reveal six bottles of ice-cold champagne. We pop open the first one and pour it in the chilled crystal glasses. I smell applesauce and pears as I bring my glass to my mouth. The bubbles dance on my tongue, and the liquid tastes creamy and decadent. As I swallow, I suddenly feel more grown up.

As we finish remaining bites of strawberries and ice cream for dessert, Todd's best friends, Andy and Mike, arrive with their dates, Carlotta and Lori. The six of us enjoy three more bottles of bubbles while sitting in the living room, talking, laughing, and debating the best time to show up at the school dance, which is only a two-minute drive away.

Since Mom told me not to worry about washing up any dishes, I blow out the cranberry candle and leave everything on the table as it is supposed to be, including opening and leaving some sparkling cider in the refrigerator. Todd puts the empty champagne bottles back in the cooler underneath the two remaining full ones, and I walk into the kitchen to wash up and dry the four wine glasses that shouldn't have been used. I place them carefully back on the shelf in the china cabinet. Everything looks in order, and we leave for the dance.

Inside the gymnasium at the high school, songs from AC/DC, Queen, Loverboy, and Chicago are blaring. A big amoeba of people moves to the beat on the dance floor. Since Todd isn't a fan of fast dances, we stand on the periphery, watching the strobe lights alter dress and suit color combinations.

Suddenly, a thought crosses my mind. I have to yell it out to be heard over Journey's "Don't Stop Believing."

"Hey, Todd, we remembered to put the ice chest back in the car, right?"

"Uh, I think. I think so. I'll go check. Be right back."

Three minutes later feels like ten. Todd rushes back toward me.

"We forgot it at your house!" He raises a hand to cover his forehead, and my gasp is inaudible given the loud music. I picture in my mind the blue plastic box with its bright white handle sitting in the middle of the living room.

"My parents will kill me."

"Let's go get it."

He grabs my hand and pulls me along with him to tell Mike we're leaving. While we pick up our pace through the parking lot of cars, Todd looks down at his watch.

"What time are they supposed to be home?"

"Ten. What time is it now?" I cross my fingers.

"It's ten minutes to ten."

"Oh my God."

The sound of my heels clapping the asphalt is deafening.

Even though my house is less than half a mile away, I know every second makes a difference. When we turn down my street and my house comes into view, I can't tell if the lighting is different or not.

"We need to go around the back side and see if their car is there first," I say while pointing where to go.

And then I see it. I let out a long sigh. They are home.

"What do you want to do, Michele?" Todd places his hand on my knee.

"I don't want to go home tonight." I close my eyes and picture being grounded for months.

"Well, you have to go home tonight, but...what...what should we do now?"

As we idle in the street, four houses away, another car pulls up alongside us. It's the other four. Todd fills them in on details, and I add that I should probably go face my consequences now.

"Let's all go," Mike says matter-of-factly.

"Really?" Just the thought is comforting.

"Yeah, it was all of us. We should just all go to your door."

After parking both cars, the five of them huddle in a group behind me on my doorstep. I press the lighted doorbell.

As the door opens slowly, my mother looks at me and everyone else with a gracious smile, her hair and makeup still perfectly intact. I'm about to speak, but she beats me to it.

"Oh, is the dance over already?"

"Uh, no. We...uh...did...did we forget something?" I finish my question by flashing my clenched teeth and holding it.

"Oh yes. You must mean the ice chest," her eyes look directly into mine.

Oh shit. I am dead meat.

But her soft voice echoes with, "Hang on. I'll get it for you."

My eyes grow large as I watch Mom casually turn around, pick it up from the middle of the living room, and hand it to Todd. With her hand still outstretched, she looks at me again and adds, "See you later on after the dance, then."

"Um, okay. I'll…I'll be home real soon."

"Bye now," she says and quietly shuts the door. Nobody moves.

"Wow. Your mom's way cool, Michele," Mike says as we walk down the steps to the street.

"No," I say, shaking my head right away. "This is totally not how she is."

Back at the dance, I can't get my mind off the replays of my mother's demeanor and the guilt digesting in my stomach. I grab a dime from my slim clutch purse and walk over to the pay phone just outside the gym doors. My father answers at the third ring with a deep, "Hello?"

"Hi, Dad. Can I, uh, can I talk to Mom?"

After a brief pause, I hear him whisper, "Our daughter."

"Hello, Michele. Everything okay?" She acts as though all is normal. I wonder for a moment if she even looked in the ice chest.

"Mom, I feel so bad. I really do. I am so sorry."

"You know, sweetie, we were kids once too. You washed up the other glasses, didn't you? Our biggest concern was drinking and driving."

"Yeah, I'm sorry. Really, I am. I can come home now if I need to."

"No. It's okay. Stay and have fun with your friends."

I place the phone back on the receiver, marvel at this surprise fortune, and feel an unusual surge of appreciation for my mother.

CHAPTER 16

APRIL 2001

D riving home with a renewed sense of hope and faith after coffee with my mom, I roll down the window and feel the breeze on my cheek. Spinning thoughts flood my mind. *What will Al think of me borrowing this money? Will it make a difference?* And then I flash on another idea: *What if I talk with my boss about the training and ask if the school district could pay the other half?*

The next afternoon, while we are walking back from the zoo, I decide to broach the topic with Al again. It's been a morning of flamingos, laughter, and ice cream cones; so it feels like a good time. More confident than nervous, I playfully toss out the question.

"Hey, honey, what would you think about me going to that eight-day training if it didn't cost anything?" I add a little skip. "Like if the cost was completely covered?" I raise my eyebrows and grin at him.

"What? What are you talking about? You said it cost about twenty-three hundred dollars." He slows down his walking pace.

"Well, what if...say...my work paid for me to go to it? So it wouldn't cost us anything. Then would it be okay with you if I went?"

Silence. More silence. And then a hesitation mixed with apprehensiveness. He shifts his gaze toward the ground and says nothing. It's as if this whole training idea is taboo now and won't be further discussed.

"Al, I don't understand." I add softly, "I thought you told Brett that this training might be good for me. I think it really could be. And if the cost is covered and wouldn't affect any funds for the new house, then?"

I look at him and wait.

Again, there is no response. No eye contact. Nothing. I wonder what has gone wrong. Through steps of silence home, I struggle to make sense of how and why something he initiated in the beginning has suddenly changed. Did he talk more in depth with Brett and learn something he didn't like? Is he not happy about me being away? Is he maybe afraid of me learning new strategies and ways to be happier and healthier? Why won't he just talk to me?

Even though I want to probe further, I do just as I've done for years now to avoid conflict. I bury my questions and say no more.

1972

I sit at the top of the stairs, my bare knees raised up to my chin, eyes fixed on the thick white barriers between my mother and me. I am six or seven and by myself, and I hear nothing. Nothing beyond the big closed double doors and nothing in the rest of the house.

My dad is downstairs in the family room in his black leather recliner next to his record player, stereo, reel-to-reel tape player, and alphabetized record collection. Headphones with a cord plugged into the stereo cover his ears. A few moments earlier when I came in from the backyard, he raised a hand to me in a distracted hello before relaxing back in sound and closing his eyes. I've been looking at these doors, wondering what's happening behind them and why she's always in there. Sometimes, I hear what I think is crying; but most of the time, I hear nothing. Silence. The only thing my dad says about times like these is, "Don't disturb your mother." I'm told she has a headache or doesn't feel well. She has a lot of headaches. Every day, it seems.

This isn't the first time I've sat here. I've found familiarity against the carpeted step, leaning against the wrought-iron railing, wishing and waiting. Sometimes, I fantasize about bursting through the doors, flinging them open, and shouting about my day, or my friends, or my teacher; but I dare not. I am a rule follower. A peacekeeper.

But today, my curiosity and loneliness get the better of me. I walk quietly up to the double doors and knock four times very softly. I am not sure, but I think I hear a quiet, "Come in." My small hand slowly turns the brass knob, opening the door gradually, exposing thick darkness on the other side. I see nothing but blackness until the door is wide enough to let in a sliver of light. My mom is in the bed, covers pulled right up to her neck. She is still and stiff on her back, her head resting on two pillows. Part of me wants to move closer and another part wants to turn and run.

"Hi, sweetie." Her voice is almost a whisper, as if she doesn't have the energy for anything beyond that. She feels like a shadow even though I can see her body right in front of me. Where has she gone? I look at the nightstand to her left. Nothing but prescription bottles and a small travel-sized alarm clock. The drawn shades completely block the summer sunlight.

"Mommy, what's wrong?"

"No, I'm okay. I just need to rest. Do you have some homework today?"

"Yes."

"Okay. Be a good girl and go do that then."

"Okay."

As she talks, her arms remain under the covers and still at her sides. Only her head moves slightly in order to see me and then shifts back into its original position. She closes her eyes. I linger for a moment and scan the corpse-like silhouette in confusion. Then I turn away and walk back through to the light side of the world, closing the door behind me and hoping my father doesn't find out I've gone where I shouldn't have.

2001

It's April, and I sit in my annual-review meeting with the superintendent, Scott Meier.

"You've had a very successful first year as principal of Jackson Elementary. I'm pleased. What areas of improvement do you see for yourself for 2001–2002?" He sits back, clasps his fingers on his desk, and maintains eye contact.

"I think I'm effective at leading the staff, but a handful of demanding parents who constantly complain have been sapping my energy. I'd like to learn some conflict resolution strategies to use with difficult people. You know, gain some updated communication skills."

I tell him about Next Level Intensive and its benefits in the corporate world, and mention that I'd like to take an upcoming training offered in July during my time off. I reach into my purse, take out the pamphlet of program information, and hand it over. I watch him scan the page and read sections with head nods of affirmation. When he turns to the final page, I suggest we split the cost.

"Yes. Do it," he says immediately. "Looks really interesting. I'd love to hear more about it when you return, okay?" He extends his hand back across the desk and adds a gracious smile.

I thank him and tell him how much it means to me to have his support and how excited I am about my soon-to-be five-minute commute after we move, and the stress it will instantly relieve.

During my long drive home, Scott's encouragement mingles with my own gut instinct, creating a stronger desire to sign up and do something good for myself. I know my mother is pulling for me too, and for some reason, that really makes a difference.

I've also been learning more about Louise Hay. She's known as one of the founders of the self-help movement. She's also a cancer survivor who attributes her healing to affirmations, visualizations, psychotherapy, and positive thinking. I bought her book, *You Can Heal Your Life,* and sure enough, it includes a list taken from her *Heal Your Body* book that suggests there is a direct correlation between dis-eases and negative thought patterns that influence health problems. She suggests "being willing to release the pattern in (my) consciousness that has created this condition." And she provides replacement thought patterns such as, "I hear with love. I listen to the Divine and rejoice at all I am able to hear. I am one with all." It's still a foreign concept for me, but there's a spark of interest that I know I need to follow.

I also know I need to go to this training. I view it as a business workshop that will help me be a happier, healthier leader and person. What I want most though is Al's blessing and support.

That night, I find him upstairs in the home office working on his computer and ask if I can come in and share about my annual review. He sits back in his chair and says, "Sure." I start with our discussions about my strengths regarding rapport with the students, parents, and community. I tell him that I was asked about areas I want to build on during the next school year, and how I shared the desire to be a better leader by knowing myself better as a leader.

"It was a perfect time to mention the NLI training and give him specific information about it. He really liked the fact that it includes communication strategies for conflict resolution and tools to lead from the heart. So he gave me the support and funds to attend. It'll cost you nothing."

"Uh, when is it?" He taps his pen on the desk a few times.

"I need to do the July 6th session during the summer break so I don't miss workdays, but I can ask your mom and mine to help with the boys on those days. Are you okay with me going?"

"Um, okay."

"Really? You are okay with it?" I repeat, wanting to make sure I heard correctly.

"Yeah," he replies, nodding his head gently yet offering no more.

"Oh, thank you, Al! Thank you! It is going to be good. I just know it!" I shriek, adding a hop of happiness and a hug that's noticeably stronger on my end.

As I turn and walk out of the room and down the stairs, I revel for a moment in my joy. *He will see. He will see how good this is for me.*

CHAPTER 17

MAY 2001

I can't believe it's been over three years since I lost my hearing. I am at my appointment with Dr. Wong, in the now all-too-familiar department of otolaryngology. Nothing seems different than my prior visits.

"There's no change to your pure tone thresholds according to your hearing test last week." Dr. Wong scans the page he's looking down at, and I hear the words *no change* play over and over in my mind. How can there still be no answers three years later? Three years.

I take a deep breath in, hold it for a moment, and contemplate if I really want to know the answer to the question I'm about to ask him. I decide on the exhale that I will. I'm ready for the truth.

"Okay, I have to ask you. Will my ability to hear *ever* come back?"

He looks into my eyes and seems to choose his words carefully.

"I don't think so. The longer it goes on, the less likely it is that it will return. I…I apologize. I can't…I can't explain why this condition exists for you."

"So then, this is just the way it's going to be." My comment is for myself more than him.

"I'm afraid so. I'm sorry. I think we will schedule six-month appointments instead of three now, unless you have any new symptoms."

I leave the building with a pink slip of paper in my hand, noting my next appointment in December.

As I walk through the congested parking lot toward my car, I recognize the familiar pressure in my chest with tears of intense frustration on standby. But I'm tired of this. Tired of fighting. Tired of false hopes. Tired of tests leading nowhere. Tired of endless struggles and whys and sobs. Right there in the middle of painted lines, unaware of anyone around me, I look up into the spring sky, drop my arms to my sides, and speak with a strong voice out loud.

"Okay, okay. If this is just the way it is supposed to be, and this is the way I am supposed to live, for whatever reason, then, well, okay. I accept this, God. I surrender."

I stand there for a few more breaths, scanning the endless skies. I feel my shoulders begin to relax. My chest starts to soften, and I hear the words of the Serenity Prayer play in my mind: *God, grant me the serenity to accept the things I cannot change. Courage to change the things I can, and the wisdom to know the difference.*

After one final long sigh, emptying myself of struggle and resistance, I decide to step forward lightly and lay down my arms of defense. I move toward my car with newfound openness to whatever lesson I'm supposed to learn. And perhaps for the first time, I choose to put some trust in the unforeseen and unknown.

A month later, it's mid-June, and Al and I are eagerly headed up to our new home. We had originally planned for a March move in, but construction delays still keep holding us back. I'm hoping this walk-through with our contractor will give us some clarity around the move-in date.

Approaching the driveway, and seeing the house raised on the hill, I notice the sun's rays beaming through the floor-to-ceiling front windows facing Folsom Lake. I search the wrap-around deck and imagine where I'll place a set of wrought-iron chairs to enjoy sunsets over the serene waters for years to come. We step across the large front yard of dirt and turn together to take in the expansive view. We're greeted by the set of old-world front doors that resembles an entrance to a castle. Inside, the smell of fresh paint on the walls hits me like a cool splash on a hot day. High ceilings, a new chandelier, the spiral staircase, and travertine floors—I'm taking it all in and am filled with anticipation of the new. Al walks with Merv, our contractor, conducting inspections of every room while I follow behind, fantasizing about furniture arrangements and hanging up my clothes in our huge walk-in closet.

"Well, overall, it looks great, Merv," Al finally says. When can we move in?"

I listen to Merv turn the daily pages of his calendar.

"Well, after adding final touches and getting a clean-up crew in here, um, I would say Friday, July 6th."

My eyes bulge but no one notices.

Unsure for a brief moment whether to say it now or not, I start with an "Umm, I—" when someone else's voice cuts in.

"The 6th it is then," Al announces and extends his hand out to Merv. I watch their firm handshake and wonder if the agreed date is just an oversight of Al's.

In the car on the drive home, I turn down Billy Idol's "Rebel

Yell" playing on the radio.

"Hey, um, July 6th? Uh, you know that's the date of the workshop I'm going to, right?"

"Well, then maybe you shouldn't go," Al shoots back.

"Huh?" I ask, bewildered by this response.

"I'm just sayin'."

"Al, I've paid for it. I'm all signed up. How about we just move in on Monday? I'm off work for the summer. I'll have all week to, you know, unpack everything."

"Nope. The house will be ready on Friday the 6th. That's the day we move in."

He turns the radio back up. I turn to stare out the window with knots twisting in my stomach and a burn in the back of my throat. I can't believe out of all the possible move-in dates, the house will be ready exactly on July 6. I want to speak more, but I feel like I need to be strategic. I wait about five minutes before reaching over to the volume knob to turn it down again.

"Al, can we just wait and move in on Monday instead of Friday? I know we're excited to finally get in the house, but I'll have to…to get to the training by 6:00 p.m. I'm staying at my parent's house for it, remember? They're gonna have the boys for the weekend. And there's a celebration at the end of the training session on Sunday, and I want you all to come. It would be so much better if we could wait just three more days."

"It'd be better for you, yeah. Look, I've been busting my ass working to get this house done, and it's done. We're movin' in." His dark-brown eyes look straight ahead at the road, and his grip on the steering wheel tightens as he accelerates.

When we turn onto Seventh Avenue and approach our house with its Sold sign staked on the lawn, I speak once more.

"Okay, Al. But that means I'll have to get everything I can done on Friday until like, uh, 5:00 p.m., and then I'm going to have to go. I can unpack more boxes on Monday."

"Whatever."

He pulls into the driveway and turns off the engine fast. Without making eye contact, he opens his door, gets out, slams it shut, and marches inside the house.

There is no room for negotiation or compromise. I know this mode. It's been happening over and over with us when I want to share my differing view on a situation he feels strongly about. I feel shut down and powerless, but I suppress the seethe of anger and submit. But as I walk slowly across the porch toward the front door, I know I will still go to this workshop.

CHAPTER 18

2014

Our ship is anchored in Paradise Bay near the abandoned scientific research structure called Almirante Brown Station. While sitting in the dining room for breakfast, I see another large colony of penguins out the window. It's snowing outside, which people say is unusual because Antarctica is actually classified as a desert. Still exceptionally blustery by regular wind standards if you ask me, the skiers are eager to get back out and find some actual powder. Everyone's buzzing about how the conditions are excellent.

Doug Stoup, the owner of Ice Axe Expeditions and an accomplished adventurer who's traveled umpteen times to Antarctica and even to the South Pole, stops by our table, chats with Gordon for a moment, and then turns to me.

"I'm going to guide your trekking group this afternoon, Michele. We'll visit the penguin rookery first and then take a walk."

I still haven't been out with the other four trekkers aboard. Again, just the thought of putting myself in the remote chance of falling into a crevasse or in the vicinity of a possible avalanche causes my heart rate to instantly increase. Doug must've sensed this.

"Michele, come here. Let me show you where we will go," he says, and I follow him onto the stern deck. When we're outside, I breathe the crisp air and listen while he points to the white scenery. He tells me we will all be roped together to climb up several switchbacks in snowshoes for a great exercise session.

"There are no crevasses, okay?" his bright blue eyes beam, and his confidence melts a little chunk of my hesitation. I want exercise after so many days on the ship, and I'm interested in going. My fear is my only barrier.

"Meet us at 12:15 at the side gate with your harness and beacon on, snowshoes and poles in hand, dressed warmly with your life vest on top." He smiles and gives me a pat on my back.

Back inside, I see Katy, Marese, and Monica, members of my group, talking together around one of the lunch tables. I approach and am greeted with warmth. Instead of pretending my vulnerability is non-existent, I tell them the truth.

"I'm feeling scared, but I'm willing to maybe try. Try being on the line today, learning what it's like. So much of this is unknown for me, and well, I don't do very well with unknowns sometimes." My voice cracks at the end, and I feel naked. I wonder if I'm revealing what these more adventurous women may perceive as silly or unnecessary, but am relieved by their immediate support.

"It's okay," Marese begins. "I totally understand. Remember, we all agreed the first day that we are a team. If it is just a ten-minute walk in fresh air, that's okay."

Katy and Monica nod their heads in agreement.

"Thanks, you guys. I so appreciate your patience with me. I'll be there at 12:15."

Back in our stateroom, Gordon affixes his avalanche beacon under two long-sleeve pieces of clothing and adds a ski jacket. I listen to him zip it up to his neck and just stare at him for a moment.

"Time for me to head back out with my group again." He claps his hands once as he holds eye contact. I feel the strong buzz of his excitement and love emanates from his eyes.

"This all looks so easy for you, honey. You really love it, don't you?" I know the answer, yet I want to learn more.

"I do. I love the fresh air and the bracing temperatures. It makes me feel healthy. Alive. The adventure of the unknown. It's energizing."

"But are you ever afraid out there?"

"Yeah, I feel fear too, but I feel secure with my group and my guides. They give me confidence. I know everything will be okay."

"Give me some of your excitement, will you? I'm working on getting up the courage to take that trek today. I'm struggling."

"You're going to be fine, sweetie. You've got great people looking out for you. Doug too. He's the head guide, Michele. He'll keep you safe. You should go." He steps toward me and gives me a big kiss. "I know you're out of your comfort zone. I'm proud of you."

After the click of the door closing behind Gordon, I begin reluctantly layering on my clothes. Wool long underwear, waterproof GORE-TEX pants, black Lucy workout jacket, Arcteryx wool under layer. I step into each leg of my harness and raise it to my hips. I grab the center loop, holding the heavy carabiner, and open and close it a few times. As Sarah instructed us, I straighten the harness so the loop faces forward, pull the side straps snugly above my hipbones, and secure it with a quick tug of the belt. I pick up the avalanche beacon, unzip the case that holds it on a shoulder harness, and turn it on. Even the quiet beep, letting me know it's actively transmitting a silent, lifesaving signal, injects adrenaline into my bloodstream.

All of this is so foreign to me. Yet I can tell that for so many on this ship, this process is as familiar as brushing their teeth. I catch the image of myself in the mirror. The woman standing wrapped in bulky warmth doesn't look familiar until I gaze further into her watery green child eyes. I want to be fearless, but how?

I close my eyes. Breathe slowly and deeply. Feel the floor beneath my wool-socked feet. Seek that heart space I've learned to connect with when I sit in silence and meditate every early morning. *C'mon. Inhale. Hold. Exhale. Where is my heart? My strength? My God?*

I grab my iPod and search my Guided Meditations playlist. I press play on a random track of Deepak Chopra's 21-Day Expanding Happiness Meditation Challenge. His soothing voice reminds me that there is no fear present when there is no separation of self from others, or from the Universe. He reminds me that I am one with everything and everyone. I concentrate carefully on each word, my heart, my light. I let the tears fall freely.

Thirty minutes later, I have dried my eyes, have all equipment in hand, and am waiting with my group-mates by the loading area. In a warm jacket beneath a waterproof outer shell, a wool hat covering my ears, goggles on my forehead, and waterproof gloves on my hands with warmers inside, I am prepared. In fact, I am uncomfortably hot and constrained. I realize I've never in my life had so many clothes on. I swallow the rise of resentment at the hassle of preparation required to venture outdoors in conditions like these. What about taking a nice run along a tropical sandy beach in shorts? So easy! I miss it. Terribly. But I let the thought pass through.

Soon, I'm standing in snowshoes at the base of a snow-blanketed mountain. I'm looking through goggles at hundreds of feathered beings in black and white suits. They waddle along right near us, unfazed by the sideways-blowing snow. While I watch a group of six penguins, one approaches. Closer than an arm's length away, she seems curious about me. I look into her eyes, her white brows prominent and fascinating—I had never thought of penguins having brows. Her bright orange beak is pointed and protruding, and her wings outstretched, revealing a clean white underside. She looks soft and friendly, and when she takes two steps closer and looks directly into my goggle-covered eyes, I wonder if she's trying somehow to convey a message. That I'm safe and watched over. That I don't need to be afraid. I stare back in awe and try to pull strength from this incredible creature.

Doug approaches as the penguin returns to her colony, the sunlight bouncing off his bright blue lenses.

"What do you think? Are you willing to try a trek?"

"Yes."

"That's fantastic, Michele."

Doug conducts an avalanche beacon test first by putting his in search mode and prompting the six of us to put our beacons in send mode and one at a time come forward so he can make sure his transceiver picks up our signal. Next, he unravels a thick long red rope and places us in a line about twenty feet apart. I am fifth on the rope. I hear a reassuring metal click as Doug attaches my carabiner to the group line and locks it.

I hold my poles tight through gloved hands and look forward to the line of rope in front of me. I am to keep it at a "relaxed smiley face" length. Not too loose to trip over, and not too tight that it pulls on Katy ahead of me.

Fluffy flakes of snow fall on my nose, and wind whips my face. The step. My breath. They are the only sounds I hear as land, glacier, sea ice, and icebergs blend into a continuous flow of desolate white. As the group's speed quickens, I concentrate on the line length and adjust my pace, settling into the momentum. My heart beats rapidly as we climb, and I notice that I'm establishing a rhythm of breath similar to when I'm running. I'm not worrying about how long our journey will be or where we are headed. I only concentrate on the sensation of foot meeting snow, the white clouds of breath from my mouth, and soft sounds of snowfall on my waterproof shell. There is no one beside me, but I see jackets ahead. I feel alone and separate, yet connected to my group.

I'm guessing we are halfway to the peak when Doug, leading our line on skis, stops, turns around, and points to me. He signals a thumb's up.

"Michele, you doing okay?" Katy in front of me turns and asks.

"Yes," I feel a genuine smile spread across my face and return a thumb's up to Doug.

Several minutes later, powerful gusts of wind kick icy grit into my face. I glance up at the mountain to the summit and watch sheets of snow traveling down in layers. Suddenly, my eyes widen and my mind takes over. *Oh no! What about an avalanche? Isn't this exactly how it happens? What if…us down here…oh God. I don't want to be buried in snow. Survival chances are slim. They say if you are buried, not to panic—just clear some space in front of your mouth if you can. Oh God. I don't want to.* My whole body suddenly wants to flee. But something stronger within squelches it. "No no no! We are *not* thinking about that, Michele. Be here. One step. One breath. That's it. Again. Step. Inhale. Exhale. Yes, good. You got this." I am talking to myself. Out loud. And it works.

I settle back into one step at a time, and soon, we reach the peak. Doug asks us to gather closer together.

"Michele," Doug's voice sounds like a yell in these conditions, "I am so proud of you!" The others smile and nod back at me too. We look at icy seas below, shrouded in white, and Doug apologizes for the poor visibility we're having at this incredible viewpoint; but that doesn't make it any less magical. The low cloud ceiling has meshed with snow. The snow falls fast, and the winds pick up, tossing it everywhere. I glance 360 degrees around and feel as if I'm spinning inside a snow globe.

During our descent, I hear the wind building behind me before I feel the shove of gusts. I grimace and stand still, putting all of my weight firmly on the snow and holding on to my submerged poles, bracing myself through the attack. I don't like this. My pulse increases, and anxiety rears its head. And then I remember. I won't disappear into white nothingness unnoticed. I am attached to a safety line. I am responsible for only me, yet part of a whole at the same time. I am not alone. Now instead of resenting the harness and rope, I see it as a gift. The thing that anchors me to something bigger.

As we descend, the visibility improves. I catch a glimpse of the penguins that from the peak resembled black specks of pepper on a blank white page. I scan my eyes over the hundreds of tuxedo-cloaked creatures for the one that visited me, but know I would never recognize her.

I am removing hand warmers from my gloves when I hear the stateroom door swing open. Gordon steps in with a vibrant smile, ski helmet still on. He holds our gaze, his hazel eyes glinting in the light. I smile back.

"Did you hear?"

"I did." He closes the door behind him. "Wow, Michele! You trekked on the continent of Antarctica today!"

"I did it, Gordon. I did it!" Tears of pride emerge.

He opens his arms, and I rush to be enveloped in them. I breathe in safety, comfort, warmth, and love. I hold this moment, us standing chest to chest, squeezing each other tight.

CHAPTER 19

JULY 2001

It's moving day. The boys are with their grandparents for the whole weekend, thank goodness, but I've been rushing around nonstop since early this morning. I'm afraid I'm going to run out of time. It's 3:30 p.m. and movers continue to unload a seemingly endless supply of packed boxes. In between giving directions to where to drop each box, I'm unpacking and organizing the kitchen items we'll need immediately. When I glance at my watch next and see hands pointing at 4:00, I jog over to the entry hall and see Al walking in with a box marked Game Room.

"I have an hour left. I'm doing the best I can, okay?"

He fails to acknowledge any words or look at me as he climbs up the stairs.

At 5:00 p.m., I'm in my closet grabbing clothes to take for the weekend. I know I need to leave now and hold true to myself and the commitment I made. I picture my mom handing me that check, my boss's handshake, and hear Brett's words replay in my mind. I zip up my overnight bag, toss extra hearing-aid batteries into my purse, and walk outside toward Al and my car.

"I gotta go, honey. I've unpacked the most important boxes. I'll call you okay, and I'll see you Sunday. I have nothing going on next week so it'll all get done. I promise."

I'm feeling flustered and anxious, but I want to kiss him goodbye. I motion to him.

"Don't go." He puts the box he's holding on the ground and stares at me.

"What?" I am intimidated by his piercing brown eyes.

"I'm not asking you, Michele. I'm telling you. Don't go."

I consider what I've just heard, and I know that even with aids in, I've heard him accurately. I'm stunned. *How can he do this to me now?*

"Al, I told you. It's paid for. I signed up a long time ago. I'm... I'm going. I have to. We've talked about this." His eyes frighten me. I turn around and feel my legs begin to shake. The ground feels as if it's shifting beneath my feet with every forward step.

"Hey," he yells. "You think I'll be there at that little 'celebration' on Sunday night? Well, think again. I'll see you Monday."

I start my car, his words carving a wound deep within me. I pull forward and out of view, but before I've reached the end of the street, I burst into tears. Loud sobs echo, and I contemplate just turning around. Forget about the personal growth opportunity and return to square boxes. Regardless of where my mind is going, it's like someone else has taken over the steering wheel. I ponder U-turns, but the car continues straight. A stronger voice emerges over my what-ifs and doubts: "We're going."

I cry the whole damn way.

As I enter a parking lot full of cars, I notice no one is outside the

Grange Hall entrance doors. I look at the clock on my dashboard and see that I'm twenty minutes late. I lean into the rearview mirror and see red puffy eyes and melted mascara reflected back. I use my pinky to wipe beneath my lashes and pinch both cheeks for some color, then grab my pad and pen and rush for the entrance.

The door to the hall squeals as I open it, and all eyes turn to look at me. Six men and three women stand in this foyer behind a set of closed doors. Some faces are friendlier than others.

"Finally! They won't let us begin until the whole group is here." The man speaking to me wears a name tag with "Brad" printed on it. I notice mine is the only one remaining on the reception table, and that my name is misspelled with two *l*'s.

"I'm sorry. Sorry I'm late," I respond to nobody in particular while forcing my lips into a tight smile.

A facilitator enters from the main hall wearing casual clothes.

"You must be Michele. Welcome to NLI."

"Thank you. I'm sorry I'm late," I say while I pin my name tag to my top anyway.

"Let's go inside and get started."

I walk behind the nine others into a large hall with nothing decorating the drab beige walls. Ten chairs with teal-green folders underneath them are lined up in a single row in the middle of the large room. A line of tables with at least eighteen chairs of people in them face us. Various shapes, sizes, hair colors, and ethnicities smile from behind papers, pens, and Post-its placed neatly in front of them. One man sits behind a large computer. This arrangement is unlike any leadership seminars I'd seen. There is no podium for a presenter, no screens for PowerPoint, and no comfortable seats at desktops for attendees. One easel with butcher paper stands to the side, but otherwise, the setting feels stark.

"Good evening and welcome. I'm Dr. Ron Wu. Please

introduce yourselves one at a time by standing up here by the easel and answering the questions we have for you."

He unwraps a sheet to display a set of four questions, each one handwritten in a different color.

Who are you?

What are you feeling?

What do you do for a living?

Why are you here?

After male participants speak, a young lady with long ringlets of brown curls wearing an olive-green Quicksilver sweatshirt gets up and takes quick steps to the front.

"I'm Christina Joy Ryan Rodrigues. I am a college student at NYU and have recently been living overseas. I am feeling anxious. Nervous about what this weekend will be like, and unsure about what's going to come out of it. But I'm excited, and I anticipate and look forward to getting to know everybody. Why am I here? Well, I'm here to figure out what I'm good at and what to focus on career-wise while working on my self-concept."

I admire her confidence and how articulate she is at a young age. She's about to step away when Ron's voice causes her to pause. "Sounds like you've already got it all figured out, Christina, and you don't really need this training. Let's add some more. Why else might you be here?"

Her narrow eyes dart from side to side, searching for a response while she seems to bristle at the added attention until she can't take it anymore and spews out, "Um, I don't like myself. I've been depressed since the age of fifteen. I need to get my act together."

"Thank you," says Ron with a nod. "You can sit down now."

I'm the eighth person to stand. I'm surprised by my sweaty palms because I've introduced myself in work situations many times to groups and not been nervous. I look at the chart and begin.

"Hi. My name is Michele. I'm feeling pretty good, and I am a—"

"Wait. You said you are feeling good. What is good?"

"Sorry, what?" I wonder if I'm hearing him correctly. Even with my hearing aids, large halls with poor acoustics are one of my most challenging situations.

"What do you mean when you say you are feeling good? What is 'good'? What is the feeling? The emotion?" He emphasizes the word "feeling" by saying it extra slow.

"Uh…um…I…" My mind races to retrieve a response. I'm flustered by the question and look up at the ceiling.

"Are you feeling nervous at all, Michele?"

"Well, I am now!" I smile at him and chuckle, an attempt to hide self-consciousness.

"You were late tonight. How do you feel about that?" He is matter-of-fact.

"Um, I'm embarrassed. Look, I'm sorry. I feel bad about holding everyone else up." My swallow is loud.

"Why were you late? "

The question stings. The harsh tone of Al's "don't go" replays in my mind. I feel tightness gnaw at my chest. The silence of the room engulfs me.

"I think I made a mistake. I don't feel like I should be here. I don't think I should've come." I look down at my feet, hoping to prevent the tears that lurk at the corners.

"Tell us why you feel you shouldn't be here."

"I just had a terrible argument with my husband. About going to this training. He told me not to go, and I left anyway. It was bad."

"And you're thinking you shouldn't be here because it has caused conflict with him?"

"Yes. Exactly."

"But what if here is exactly where you need to be?" he asks and nods once.

I search for a response and what comes out is, "Hmm, maybe. I don't know."

"Well, Michele, it looks like your training has already begun."

Back in my seat with the others, I listen with curiosity as we're told that note taking won't be necessary, and we will spend time journaling later. Rather than sitting in chairs listening, there will be a variety of group experiential exercises. There will be songs to listen to and quotes to ponder. We will also spend time individually with our two assigned coaches to identify and set goals for what we'd like to work on and what we'd like to get from attending the three-day session.

During a quick exercise to pair each of us up with a "buddy"—another participant we will support and receive support from for the duration of the program—I select Nancy who is almost six feet tall, large-boned and fair-skinned, with flowing long strawberry-blond hair and bright orange lipstick. Nancy exudes confidence and a carefree spirit. She's from Los Angeles, and I am drawn to her upbeat, extroverted, and humor-filled personality along with her affinity for the beach.

One of the first topics covered is about feelings. As I look over the paper handed out and scan the list of extensive emotions, I notice how many more feelings there are beyond mad, sad, happy, afraid, and ashamed. Feelings like grounded, forgotten, cherished, and restless surprise me. "Good," of course, is not on the list. And neither is "bad."

"We will be talking a lot about the defenses we put up to hide ourselves when overwhelming or unpleasant feelings surface, particularly in times of anxiety or during conflict." Ron scans the room and pauses. "Ways we show up with others."

Nancy breaks the solemnness in the room. "Well, I never hide who I am, although the general consensus seems to suggest that I should." She laughs with gusto, following words delivered like a true stand-up comedian.

Leadership team members immediately use her comment as a perfect example of using the cloak of self-deprecating humor to conceal what more truthful feelings may exist beneath the surface. Nancy accepts the feedback with grace, sharing with us that the intensity of the energy in the room intimidated her, thus evoking her comment. Others open up as a result during interactions with staff who coach us through simple role plays to identify defenses. "I think I use a lot of sarcasm and attack when I am provoked," states Brad. More discussions continue.

Christina adds, "I think I tell people what they want to hear."

The room full of honesty and self-reflection feels peculiar to me, but I find a sense of freedom when sharing the truth.

"I realize I tend to stay silent, or agree, or apologize, and smile to mask intense feelings," I say.

After an evening-snack break, the ten of us sit in a line of folding chairs, facing the longer panel of coaches, buddies by our sides. In the center of the room, a spotlight of sorts shines down on a piece of blue tape on the floor. We learn that each of us will be called one at a time to stand on it for the final exercise of this first evening, something called Dark Mirrors. I squeeze the side of my folding chair when I witness Brad's eyes grow wide after a coach delivers the words, "I experience you as A Snake-Oil Salesman."

Christina, baby-faced with plump cheeks, chews on her bottom lip while she stands and listens to hers. "I experience you as A Constant and Convenient Chameleon." I see her pull the cuff of her sleeves down over her fisted hands before the next one. "I experience you as A Shrinking Violet." When she walks back to her seat, she inserts both hands into the front pouch pocket of her sweatshirt and stares down at her black sneakers with the zebra-print tongue.

My heart pounds loudly in my chest when my name is called. I hear my sandals echo across the hardwood floor and stop when they find the mark. The stone faces in front of me don't seem like the same people seated there earlier, but they are. I flash a polite smile, but it is not reciprocated by any of them. My arms feel heavy at my side, and I'm unsure how or where to place my hands.

The lead facilitator speaks first, remaining expressionless but without venom. "Michele, I experience you as A Smiling Imposter."

One after the other, I receive their "experiences" while my right forefinger inconspicuously picks at the cuticle on my thumb.

"I experience you as An Imploding Heart/Lung Machine."

"I experience you as A Barbie Doll."

"I also experience you as A Barbie Doll."

"I experience you as A Rescuing Doormat."

The room suddenly feels cold as the different voices deliver their messages. I squirm and fidget. There are seven more to go.

"I experience you as Polly Perfect People Pleaser."

"I experience you as A People Pleaser."

"I experience you as A Controlled Barbie Doll."

Several tears escape. I wipe them away with haste.

"I experience you as Politically Correct."

"I experience you as A People-Pleasing Doormat."

The skin surrounding my nose and above my lip is tingling as watery eyes follow the final three. I inhale a shallow breath.

"I experience you as A Scared Little People Pleaser."

"I experience you as An Emotional Sponge Wiping Up Everyone's Spills."

"I experience you as A Smiling Prisoner."

Every panelist has spoken, and my feet beg me to flee. And then I remember the directions given at the start. I need to turn around and face my nine group-mates. They too will give me feedback of how they experience me. I swallow as I turn reluctantly and look into their eyes. I think I see pity and gear myself up to hear more without falling apart. The facilitator tells them to take turns going down the row. Some of them look almost as uncomfortable as me.

"I experience you as a vulnerable, fearful people pleaser." Nancy then looks down at her lap.

"I experience you as a frightened person." His eyes show care.

"I experience you as fearful loving." He looks to the next person.

"I experience you as an emotional sponge who's not loving self." She smiles at me.

"I experience you as someone who has a heart that's scattered." He is matter-of-fact.

"I experience you as someone who has an incredible heart and wants to save the world." He shrugs his shoulders at the end.

"I experience you as a mother." His voice cracks at "mother."

"I experience you as unaware of amazing emotions within." Christina's eyes send love.

"I too experience you as a people pleaser." He is matter-of-fact.

After being directed to return to the seat with my group, Nancy squeezes my knee and looks downward. I hear all the phrases repeat over and over in my head. They're loud, and I want to silence them.

It's after midnight when the exercise is complete for all of us. Before being dismissed, we're handed a sheet of paper titled Dark Mirrors Homework to complete tonight when we get home. It will be collected when we return in the morning at 8:00 a.m.

The ten-minute drive to my parents' house is traffic free, and I'm relieved when I walk upstairs into the bedroom that's been mine since I was twelve. The same white furniture greets me, and when I plop down on my familiar double bed, it's a refuge of safety. I'm exhausted and don't want to do the homework, but I know I won't want to wake up in less than six hours. I change into my nightshirt and prop myself up in bed with pillows. The instructions say to write at least half a page for each of the five questions about reactions to hearing Dark Mirrors. My pen moves across the page like a jaguar after its prey. When I'm done, I toss my pen on the nightstand, set my alarm, and turn out the light.

Back at the hall at 8:00 a.m. on Saturday morning, all of our written responses are collected. While I watch the stack of white papers moving away, I'm relieved to be rid of the Dark Mirrors. On a white board hanging up on the wall is the quote of the day: I want to unfold. Let no place in me hold itself closed, for where I am closed, I am false.—Rainer Maria Rilke

Two facilitators emerge from behind the closed doors to the main hall. One of them is the man who gave me the name of Imploding Heart/Lung Machine. He looks at me and calls me over. When I approach, I see he's holding my homework.

"We're asking you to rewrite your responses to questions three and four. Instead of writing at least half a page, you wrote just several sentences. We need more. Do them now and I'll collect them in twenty minutes."

He outstretches his hand with the papers. Bubbling lava runs from my stomach up into my throat, but I reach out and take them. The door closes behind him with a sharp click.

You've got to be fucking kidding me.

Nancy approaches me and puts one hand on my shoulder. "Are you okay, buddy?"

"No. No, I'm not okay. I don't understand." My voice is shaky, and I feel hot inside, which frightens me. "After all that, now I can't even answer questions right."

"Look, I think it could help to write down everything you're feeling right now. All of it."

"He said I was an imploding heart-and-lung machine. What the fuck?"

"You feel for others. I see that. But do you feel for *you?*" Her words are soft and slow.

"What?" I squint at her.

"I think that's what they're offering you the opportunity to look at. Are you there for yourself or do you collapse inward?"

I stare into her hazel eyes and search for clarity.

"Write it, Michele. All of it."

I move to a quiet corner and look around. Several participants are reading papers in their folders, one eats an apple, and others chat. I pull out a clean sheet of binder paper and begin rewriting my responses. My words this time are more detailed, thorough, and honest, like Nancy suggested.

> The Dark Mirrors that hurt me the most were Smiling Imposter and Barbie Doll. I feel empty and "found out" or "discovered," and I am angry about that. I feel the intense need to make sure everything on the surface looks okay. To have people discover and label this intention is devastating. I sense danger close

by and a fierce need to avoid it.

I am concerned and confused about being given the Imploding Heart/Lung Machine comment. The machine part suggests there isn't a person here, and I can't understand how I come across as a machine. This makes me wonder if I'm cold or not alive. I feel like I am able to feel—especially during a crisis or if someone else is in need. But maybe I'm not there for myself. I am angry about that. It appears that people in this training don't approve of me and that hurts. When someone tells me I am an Imploding Heart/Lung Machine—then my gosh, I must not be okay. And not being okay is my biggest fear.

Soon we start our work with our two personal coaches. I have one female lead coach named Gloria, and a male secondary coach named Dean. They help me dissect my responses and feelings about the Dark Mirrors. I'm candid, sharing how uncomfortable and vulnerable I feel. They explain that the exercises are intended to help me learn some important truths about myself and who I am.

Gloria begins, "I want you to close your eyes now. Go back and feel that vulnerable place within when you were listening to the dark mirrors. Hear them again. Over and over. Are you back in that space yet?"

"Yes, but can you speak a bit louder please? It's hard to hear you sometimes."

"Of course. What do you hear them say?"

"Doormat. And scared little people pleaser."

"And hearing those words, what do you feel?" Her voice remains calm and warm.

"I'm sad. I feel hurt and lonely, and I feel like I just want to go run and hide."

"Why do you want to run and hide?"

"Because I...I don't matter. I don't feel worth anything."

"Have you felt those same feelings before last night?"

"Um, yeah, I have." A sharp stabbing pain arrives in my chest.

"Okay. Now go back to the first time you remember feeling these very same feelings.

An image arises on the screen behind the lids of my eyes.

"How old are you and where are you?"

"I'm six. And I'm sitting at the top of the stairs in my house, staring at closed white double doors."

CHAPTER 20

JULY 2001

By lunchtime on the second day of the course, it's very clear that this training will not just be about my job as an elementary school principal. Instead, I will spend hours getting to know a hurt, defensive, scared, lost, and embarrassed little girl and her core wounds. The little girl within, holding a full spectrum of feelings I've silenced. I locked her away years ago, but now she's been unexpectedly woken up by the prods and pokes of this training. All she longs for is safety, security, and love.

My introduction to meditation begins with a five-minute meditation. I've heard of people that begin their day in quiet each morning, but I've never known how you really do it. I don't like closing my eyes lately either. Not having good hearing, shutting off the sense of sight as well elicits feelings of panic.

The facilitator begins by asking us to take three deep breaths through our nose, holding at the top of the breath, and then exhaling slowly through the mouth.

"Now close your eyes and ask yourself, 'What main emotion am I feeling right now?' Think of one word." *Vulnerable.*

"After you have that word, ask yourself, 'What do I need to do about this emotion today?'" *I need to allow myself to feel it and not push it away.*

"Next, ask yourself, 'What is my intuition leading me to do with the day before me?'" *Be honest and truthful when you feel vulnerable, and believe you're meant to be here.*

After we open our eyes, we're given a piece of paper titled The Five Minute Daybreak Meditation by Dr. Selden B. Marth. We're encouraged to make thirty-one copies, one for each day of the month, and do the meditation daily for one month, writing our brief answers down after each question and returning to eyes closed for the next.

"It can be interesting to review what you've written after a month of practice. You can then meditate on whatever recurring patterns you find."

I feel a spark of motivation to start practicing daily meditation and observe the changes I experience.

The next morning, it's my turn to participate in an exercise called Follow the Thread. I've been asked to select a recent emotionally charged scenario to delve into with two leadership team facilitators. I stand in the middle of the room between them.

"What are you feeling in this moment, Michele?"

"I'm feeling nervous." I move my feet a couple of times to

settle in as the whole room observes.

"Tell us about a recent experience you've had feeling intense emotions."

"Well, all day on Friday, my husband Al and I were involved in moving into our new house. He knew I was going to this training because it has been planned for months and already paid for. I let him know I needed to leave at five o'clock. When it came time to leave and I was heading to my car, he stopped me and told me not to go. Then he said, 'I'm not asking you. I'm telling you.'" My voice sounds shaky.

"How did that make you feel?"

"Shocked, angry, and then afraid."

"Close your eyes and feel in your body those words: 'I'm not asking you. I'm telling you.' Do you feel that?"

"Yes."

"Where in your body do you feel it?"

"It's in my chest." I let out a loud sigh with it.

"Put your hand on your chest and breathe into that feeling. Allow it to be there. Can you describe this feeling in your chest?"

"It's…it feels really tight."

"If you could give it a number of intensity between one and ten, what would it be?"

"Seven. It really hurts."

"Okay. Yes, stay with that. You're doing great. So breathe into that level seven of pain and let it grow to an eight, maybe even a nine. It's tight, I know. What else does it feel like?"

"It's a sharp, deep pain. It makes me feel like I can't move. Like a vice. Like I'm being squeezed and it might crush me." My breath quickens.

"So stay with that feeling in your chest, of feeling squeezed and crushed, and breathe into it. I imagine you have felt this feeling

136

before. Have you?"

"Yes." I nod several times.

"Okay, so stay with the intense feeling of being squeezed by a vice in your chest. I want you to go back in time and follow this same feeling back, all the way to the very first time you felt this feeling. It'll come to you. Just keep going back while you stay with the feeling. Go back to that first time you felt this. Are you there?"

"Yes."

"How old are you?"

"I think I am six or seven." I see her image clearly.

"All right, stay with you at the age of six or seven when you feel this feeling. Where are you and what are you doing?"

"I'm in the house where I grew up, in the hallway. My dad is really mad. My brother and I have been having fun playing, but he says we're being too loud and tells us to stop it and be quiet because we're going to disturb my mom."

"Okay. He says, 'Stop it. Be quiet.' Is that right?"

"Yes. And he has a mean look on his face. He scares me. I can't say anything back to him. If I do, I will make him more mad."

"What will happen if you make him more mad?"

"He will smack me and then ignore me, not speak to me at all. I will be alone and invisible."

"So you'll be banished to a jail of silence, and feel alone and ignored?"

"Yes." I begin to cry

"So you're six years old. Stay with that six-year-old self. What did you tell yourself about you in that moment?"

"That I am a disappointment. That I never say or do anything right." More tears fall from my eyes, and my voice trails off

"Say that again."

"I am a disappointment. I never say or do anything right."

"Now I want you as adult Michele to look at six-year-old Michele standing there in her house crying because she doesn't feel like she can speak up. She thinks she is a total disappointment, and she can't do or say anything right. Can you see her? Look deep into those eyes of hers. Is that what's really true about her?"

"No. She does a lot of things right. She's got a huge heart."

"Keep looking into her eyes. Can you tell her what is true about her?

"She's not a disappointment. She has a huge heart, and she says a lot of things right. I love her, and I want to hug and hold her like a loving, caring parent ought to do.

"Is there anything else you want to say to her?"

"That I will be there for her when she needs me, and I'll protect her. That she is worthy of love."

"Okay. Now look into her eyes again and say to her, 'I will be there for you whenever you need me. I'll protect you. I love you.' Good. Can she hear you? Does she believe you?"

"Yes. She's happy about that." I sniff twice.

"Will you commit to always being there for her when she needs you?"

"Yes."

"Now slowly come back from that memory. Back to this present moment as an adult with your eyes open." I see other moist eyes in my row of group-mates.

"Michele, can you describe how you're feeling now."

"I feel compassion. I understand. I see where those feelings come from." I wipe salty trails from my cheeks.

The other facilitator suggests I find a symbol to help me remember the knowingness of being worthy, deserving of love, and free to speak up and have my own opinions. A pink heart-shaped image comes immediately to mind. I feel it in my chest as a replacement for that vice-like pain. I breathe into those qualities and decide I can touch my heart and remember softness any time those old feelings surface.

I am a disappointment.
I always say and do the wrong thing when I want to be helpful.
I am too sensitive, and I get my feelings hurt too often.

My two coaches help me identify these negative core beliefs and reframe and replace them with an affirmation, which I write on an index card. I will tape this card to my bathroom mirror and recite it regularly as one of my practice tools during the ten-day window before the five-day session. I hold up the index card and see the words staring back at me.

I am a secure, worthy woman, and I trust my own instincts.

It's Sunday afternoon, and our three-day session is coming to a close. We sit as a whole group listening to details regarding this evening's celebration. Some participants will have family members here; others have invited friends. Al and I haven't spoken since he told me not to expect his attendance, and he hasn't left me any messages on my cell phone.

One of the facilitators asks for a show of hands from people who don't have anyone coming. I raise mine. My group-mate, Howard, a man at least ten years older than me, looks at me with surprise.

"Michele, uh, I know you said your husband isn't coming, but didn't you say your parents live close by? Aren't you staying with them? How come they aren't coming?"

"I didn't say anything to them about coming."

"But why?"

"Well, I didn't think they'd be comfortable, and my son, Trevor, is with them. Anyway, it's kind of late now. The celebration is in an hour and a half."

"Well, I'd like to suggest you call them and invite them anyway. They can decide if they don't have enough time to get here. And in case there's some element of feeling non-deserving in your rationale, you're worth showing up for. Seriously, would it hurt to just ask them?

Howard's words penetrate deep. At the break a few minutes later, my coach asks me what feelings arise when I consider making the call. I tell her I feel fear. Fear of how uncomfortable I might feel if they see all the deep work I'm doing here. The blatant truths, all the vulnerability, the raw and real expressions of emotion. I feel guilty about exposing secrets too. I remember my dad telling me as a child that what happens in our home shouldn't be shared— that it's nobody's business but ours. No one ever knew my mother was severely depressed. And even today, she still suffers from dark bouts of depression that are never discussed. The last layer of fear I hold is: what if I ask my parents to come and they say no? The rejection would deepen my wound of hurt. I would have no one. I would rather just not expect anyone to be there and not be disappointed. She listens with caring eyes and nods. I feel heard.

"I'm wondering, Michele, if you can feel that fear and face it anyway. You're making assumptions on their part. You're in fear of what-ifs. Until you call and ask, you don't know."

When Gloria walks away, I fish my phone from my purse, take a brave breath, and dial. My dad answers and tells me my mom and Trevor are taking a nap. I tell him that I realize I hadn't asked them earlier, but that if they could come, I would like to invite them to tonight's celebration at six o'clock. Dad says he'll check with Mom in a little while, and if they can, they will be there.

I'm surprised to hear a twinge of interest in his voice.

When I hang up, I feel a lift in my mood. I walk over to Howard, thank him for everything he said, and tell him I'm glad I told my parents I'd like them to come whether they actually do or not.

It's 5:50 p.m., and I'm standing in a circle, arm in arm with the nine other participants. Our eyes are closed, and we sway together gently side to side while being led through a guided meditation. I listen with concentration to the facilitator's words of inspiration, affirmation, and comfort. When the meditation comes to a close, we're instructed to turn around slowly and open our eyes.

Mom, Dad, and little Trevor stand in front of me. My eyes and mouth open wide. I rush to embrace them all.

CHAPTER 21

2014

I look out the window from our stateroom. Another morning of white. White air, white mountains, white clouds, white wave caps, white sky. Brightness bounces off the iceberg tips. While it is light for many hours, it is light without sunshine—a flat, white light.

Because of the low cloud ceiling and poor visibility, Zodiac tours are the only activity available this morning. There are seals to spot and a shipwreck still frozen in ice from a century ago. Gordon is excited to participate, as are many of the other adventurers who seem stir crazy and eager to get off the boat. A cozy day inside with a cup of tea and a good book sounds good to me, but because he wants to go, I am layering on my clothes again, now quick and proficient at this routine. In our stateroom, Gordon plays some Jackson Browne songs on his iPhone. He sings along, and I am comforted by the sound of his deep, strong voice. Even though he is ten years older than I am, we have similar tastes in music and have seen lots of musicians in concert together, Jackson Browne included.

The departure gate is crowded with bundled-up enthusiasts. The line moves quickly. I am trying to get my waterproof gloves on over my liners. As I tug at my gloves and work my fingers into their slots, cold gusts blow against my face. I glance out at white-capped turbulence. I feel flustered and rushed. My gloves aren't on properly. My fingers on both hands won't straighten, and I worry I don't have enough time to fix them before I'm called to board.

"You go. I'm not gonna go," I announce to Gordon through my goggle-covered face.

"But wait. I'll help."

I don't want to go anyway. I turn and move like a fish swimming upstream through the crowd of hats, balaclavas, and goggles. It feels absurd to me that all these people want to wait in a long line to venture out into freezing conditions. I roll my eyes. Once again, I'm the one who doesn't belong.

As I turn to climb up the stairs, I take a breath of relief and remove my goggles and hat.

I'm at the top, feeling free, when I bump into the broad chest of Johnny, a 6'4" snowboarder with long brown wavy hair, sapphire-blue eyes, and a warm smile housed within a mustache and beard. He's with his roommate and friend, John, who has a raccoon tan-line from all the skiing and adventuring.

"Hey, aren't you going the wrong way?" Johnny asks.

"I decided I am not going."

"What? Why not?" John joins in.

"Well, I...I...had a problem—my gloves." I realize I sound ridiculous.

"C'mon. Come with us. Let's go," John says, putting a hand on my shoulder.

"But I—"

"Oh, c'mon. Just put your outer gloves on. I'll hold your liners in case." Johnny takes my liners and puts them in his pocket while he steps forward.

"Next week, you won't be able to do this, you know," says John.

His words linger. He's right. Am I going to let a stupid pair of gloves get in my way?

"All right," I respond. My gloves slide on with surprising ease this time. I follow them both down the stairs.

When I board, I sit next to Johnny. As I glance up, Gordon is goggle- and hood-covered, sitting directly across from me. We are both surprised to see each other.

"Oh, hi! What are you doing here?" he says with a big smile, reaching over to pat my knee.

"We found her trying to escape at the top of the stairs. Brought her with us," Johnny says in a joking tone.

I'm still not convinced I will enjoy this excursion. The ride is bumpy, and freezing water occasionally sprays up against my back. My grip is tight on the outer rope along the rubber boat. The driver and marine biologist, Santiago, navigates the seas, pointing out crabeater and Weddell seals, icebergs, Adélie penguins, and the frozen shipwreck. It's been fifteen minutes, and I'm just now beginning to breathe normally again. I feel the crisp air through my nostrils as I inhale, and after exhaling, I open my mouth to taste some falling snow. Ice crackles serenely around us. Santiago cuts the engine and explains the difference between glacial ice and sea ice. Afterward, we float in silence for a few minutes.

I scan the iceberg-filled surroundings, taking in gorgeous shapes and sculptures that even Walt Disney couldn't possibly create. I stare at these unusual formations created by waves and the varying temperatures of the ocean. Jagged edges on display, carvings like scars from past experiences, points, peaks, and pristine exteriors with turquoise shimmers. All of this above the sturdy, dark, hidden layers lurking below the surface. Beauty and harshness. Showing off and hiding away at the same time.

I ponder the excavations I've done to heal some of the shadowed parts of myself in order to no longer be fearful of them. I stare a few moments longer and consider how the icebergs teach me about illusion. The top portion, the unique formations of wonder and beauty, catches our attention while the unseen, unknown depth below the surface, can instantly destroy a sailing ship.

As the Zodiac's motor starts and we move through sea ice again, Gordon looks at me, gives two thumbs up, then blows me a kiss. Johnny leans over and says, "Want some good news?" I nod.

"I can see the ship."

For the remaining ride, I breathe deeply and feel glad I came on this excursion after all. The Antarctica sculptures, the sea ice, the silence. The reminder to be present in the moment.

The next day, Gordon and I are in our stateroom relaxing on our beds. He's been telling me all about his experience skiing earlier. "We spent a good two hours making our ascent, which was challenging at times. But to unhook from our rope and get first dibs on untracked, untouched snow, it was mind-blowing!" I listen to his tones of exhilaration while he provides the moment-by-moment recap. I hold eye contact and nod along.

Crackles interrupt him and an announcement starts, "Ladies and gentlemen, get ready for the *Polar Plunge*! It will be held in thirty minutes. Put your swimsuit on—or not—and cover yourself with the robe in your staterooms. Meet downstairs in the loading-platform hallway."

My eyes widen while Gordon's expression reminds me of a Cheshire cat.

"Wanna do it with me?" He beams at me, and I laugh out loud.

"Oh my God. *No!* Are you really going to jump in freezing waters?"

"*Yes*, I am doing it!" I can tell from his expression that he will. He shows no hesitation, no concern for temperature. Just the thought of it makes my hands feel tingly. I watch him change into blue and white swim trunks, and affix a black harness strap to his hairy chest. "I'll take my GoPro with me!" He grabs a white robe hanging in our bathroom, places his arms through the sleeves, ties it around his stomach, and rests his hands on his hips. I giggle and start the process of adding layers again, including a hat and scarf. On the way out, I grab a packet of hand warmers, my camera, and gloves.

Forty-nine white-robed guests write their name down to participate and stand in a line together. *Forty-nine out of one hundred and two*, including my trekking buddies, Marese and Katy. I tell them, Gordon, and several others that I will take the job of playing photographer from the fourth deck to capture their craziness on camera.

I push open the heavy ship door to falling flakes and a gust that makes me shiver. I walk carefully across the slippery deck and hold onto the railing. When I glance below, I see gray metal steps with handrails leading down to a small platform. Two guides wait, holding a thick ring of rope, while two other guides are positioned in a Zodiac boat floating off to one side. I find the most strategic location to take great photographs and practice on those at the front of the line.

Each polar plunge participant emerges barefoot in swimwear, many with shoulders pulled up to their ears. After climbing carefully down to a platform at the water's edge, they're met by a guide who wraps a thick rope tightly around their waist. After the rope is secure, the guide directs them to jump or dive in the dark blue wavy waters on the count of three.

I notice many men who say nothing before they jump, canon ball, or dive in. The handful of women brave enough to walk outside emerge with shaky voices saying things like, "Oh my gosh, what am I thinking? It's freezing out here." Marese is one of them. She timidly jumps in as if to avoid getting her hair wet but doesn't succeed. She climbs out shrieking and shaking. I take her picture, yell, cheer, and holler for her.

Gordon is about the fifteenth to go. As he emerges, my heart flutters and I call out, "Wahooo! Gor-don!" He pauses, turns his head, looks up at me, and flashes a prepared-to-do-this thumbs-up. He raises his arms straight up in the air as the rope is placed around his waist and secured with a locking carabiner. Snowflakes fall as I zoom in on him with my lens.

Letting out the line of rope, the guide motions for Gordon to step to the edge. "On the count of three. One, two, three!" Gordon jumps confidently into the frigid Southern Ocean with a loud splash. He's fully submerged while pieces of ice float by. He surfaces and swims expertly back fast toward the platform, where the guide pulls him in. I capture every moment until he climbs on deck. I hear his groans until applause rings out, mine included. He looks immediately to me after climbing two steps up and shakes a clenched fist of victory in the air with a huge smile and a strong,

147

deep, "Yeah!"

When Gordon moves out of view into the covered area, the staff congratulates him with a towel and a shot of vodka. Several minutes later, he emerges on the deck beside me in his robe and flip flops with outstretched arms, a pink face, and wet hair.

"How do you like me now, baby?" he asks triumphantly.

"Hahaha. I love you!" I lean over and kiss his frosty lips.

"I love you too, Michele. And I'm so glad you're here with me."

The trip of a lifetime very few get to experience, he had told me six months prior. Indeed, he was right.

CHAPTER 22

AUGUST 2001

I'm grateful that all ten of the training participants are staying in the same hotel just a short distance from the Grange Hall for the second part of the workshop. Nancy is my roommate, and she's starting to feel like an older sister. We all have breakfast together each morning. I think back to our first day when I walked into a room full of strangers and can't believe how close we've become. Sharing fears, vulnerabilities, and hurts in such an open environment has bred a deep trust between us in a short amount of time. In some ways, these nine people know me better than my closest friend and family.

During the last ten days, I had felt excited about organizing kitchen cupboards, setting up new bedrooms with Brennan and Trevor, and shopping for new sheets and comforters the day our new king-sized bed was delivered. I'd wake up in the morning feeling peaceful and calm as I read my affirmation and glanced out at the glistening waters of the lake.

But a tension exists in our house that we are ignoring. Even though Al's physically there, he's been lodging in his own world, with little interest in interacting with me. I feel shut out. He didn't once ask me how the training was for me or how I'm doing at all. Is he punishing me? I attempt to give and send love no matter how he acts and try to stay in my own place of centeredness, but it's not easy. I notice I'm feeling lonely and resentful. I know I still have a large amount of work to do on myself these next five days.

All ten of us are asked to stand up in a straight line side by side during this evening's session for another experiential exercise. Dr. Wu gives instructions.

"One participant at a time during their turn will stand directly in front of each group-mate for about thirty seconds and hold eye contact with them. After this period, each member in the row will announce whether they experience the participant standing in front of them as a giver or a taker. The decision is based upon the energetic connection felt along with what you've observed of one another these past days. By looking deeply into another's eyes, we can sense if someone is giving, or if they show up with more desire to receive. We experience this out in the world even with strangers. A sense that some people would give you the shirt off their back while others wouldn't. So let's begin."

I'm uncomfortable right away. I'm anxious about being judged, but I also feel reluctant to tell someone else they are a taker because I don't want to hurt them.

It's my turn. I stand in front of the first of my nine group mates. After about fifteen seconds, I hear and lip-read the word "giver." I move to the right and stand in front of another. After twenty seconds, I get my second label: "giver." I stand in front of the next and the next, gazing into different heights, sets, and colors of eyes. As I reach the end, I feel great relief. I've had nine "giver" responses. I feel as if I aced this test. I grin, pleased with myself.

"Michele, how do you feel about being a giver?" Dr. Wu's question is matter-of-fact.

"I feel happy about it. I think I am a giver."

"So you see this as something positive then?

"Um, yes. Absolutely." *Why wouldn't it be?*

"Would any of Michele's group-mates like to add some comments about her having a hundred percent giver label?"

I'm confused when I see heads nod in agreement. Christina raises her hand high in the air, and Dr. Wu instructs her to look directly at me and give her feedback.

"Michele, when you don't receive, you deny the gift of the giver. It makes me really sad. I know you're a giver, but I'm afraid you're going to give it all away. There will be nothing left for you."

I am stunned. I feel as empty as a tire that's blown out while traveling in the fast lane of a freeway. A surge of sadness fills my whole body. A loud knock to the door of my heart jolts me awake. And I realize the deep feeling I've held for three years now that I'm somehow dying inside might not be so far from the truth.

The hall smells of sweat this afternoon. I've heard gut-wrenching cries, fits of shouting and rage, and rhythms of whiffle bats pounding on mats. I've done all of these myself in my own floor work too. Long days into late nights, I work through many issues I've identified with my coaches. I've been thinking about my health and hearing. About what perhaps is blocking me from using my ears to listen to true sound.

"Let's try a guided visualization," my coach, Gloria, offers. She invites me to lay down on a mat with a pillow under my head. I stretch out and look at her for instruction, unsure of what to expect.

"Just relax, Michele. Take a long, deep, cleansing breath in, and then release it. Good, do that again and close your eyes this time on the exhale. Nice. Now let the tension out of your shoulders relax even more."

I don't like my eyes closed. I can't hear her very well when she speaks this soft. Plus, she's positioned on my left side, closer to the ear that isn't as strong even with hearing aids in. I open my eyes and look at her. "It's hard for me to hear you. Can you switch to my better side and talk a bit louder?"

Gloria nods and smiles, "Of course." She steps around my head and sits on the floor beside my right ear. She directs me to close my eyes again and puts a gentle hand on my shoulder. I still feel antsy. Thick blackness fills the space beneath my eyelids. I want to open them again, and I wonder perhaps if peeking will help ease the fear of somehow being swallowed up in darkness. I strain to listen to her tell me that she will ask me to picture some things in my mind and then ask me some questions about what I see.

"A couple more deep breaths, okay? Settle in softer. There you go. I want you to visualize what it's like to travel inward, into your body. Through the exterior of your skin into the organs, tissues, and pathways. Let's travel to your ears. Take your time to go there, and let me know when you've arrived at your right ear."

I repeat the instruction to myself silently to travel to my ears, but inside the impermeable black, there is resistance and anxiousness. I feel as though I'm about to visit a foreign place. And the unknown has never felt like a friend of mine. My breath quickens and Gloria must notice.

"What do you see, Michele?"

"It's just all black. Thick black. And all clogged up, like in a huge chunk. I feel afraid. I don't…like it."

"It's okay. You're safe to stay there. Just observe it and look around for some light that wants to appear, even if just a speck. Stay with it. There's no rush. See what you notice."

I'm searching in every direction around the blanket of gunk, but there is no light. No change. I take another in-breath and my exhale sounds like a sigh of exasperation.

"I can't find any light."

I'm ready to open my eyes and escape this horrible aloneness. Maybe visualizations aren't for me.

"Just be there with it. And allow in the light. I'm right here beside you." She squeezes my shoulder gently and leaves her hand there.

I take another breath and search again for any glimmers. I move my eyeballs around the periphery of the closed quarters. I scan my screen of dark again, and all of a sudden, it catches my gaze—a tiny dot of golden light.

"Oh, I see something. It's a teeny dot up toward the right."

"Yes. Breathe into that dot. Watch it grow as you give it some air and invite it in."

I follow Gloria's words and focus on my breath. I feel air tickle the inside of my nose. With subtle shifts, the dot becomes a small solid ball of golden-white. Its presence starts to dissolve bits and pieces of the darkness, and I notice warmth move in. Not only warmth from the glow, but also within my bloodstream.

I continue to listen to Gloria's soothing voice that encourages the expansion of light into my ear canal. I picture the complex labyrinth of my inner ear; it's like a snail of intricate tubes. I notice the light has taken on some bluish tints as it rushes through each tube at the right of my skull, removing barriers of black as it travels.

I hear a new soft voice within guide more rays of light into my brain and throughout my entire head. I picture light cleansing the space within a tube-like highway from my right ear to my left. The darkness starts to dissipate. The longer I linger here, the more light sweeps into every crevice.

When Gloria asks me to tell her what I'm seeing now, I feel overwhelming joy and attempt to describe the scene.

"Clarity has replaced clogged, and it's so beautiful. I can see a line of light from one ear to another that runs through my skull with no blockages."

"Bask in your light, Michele. Breathe fully into it."

I remain with the expansion and that same subtle voice tells me that it's safe to hang out here for a while. I watch and feel, and let light shower over me.

When Gloria asks me to open my eyes about three minutes later, her nurturing face is a warm greeting.

"How was that for you?"

"I'm, oh my gosh, I'm amazed. I've never done anything like that before. I can still feel the clearness, the tunnel of light I saw."

"You can come back to this part of you anytime. You can visualize healing light within whenever you want. It may be helpful to do it more."

"I will. I definitely will."

It's a promise to myself that I keep.

As the last moments of the training come to a close, I feel a blast of aliveness. I feel better about myself than ever before. I've grown close to all the other participants in the group, but in particular, Nancy and Christina. I know I have a new family of support that will continue to encourage me to live authentically.

The Sunday celebration has begun. We stand again in our "love circle," as we call it, all ten of us huddled close, standing and swaying arm in arm while being led through a guided meditation. Our eyes are closed, the lights dim. I savor the strong bonds I feel—a level of depth and truth I've never experienced before. As the meditation comes to a close, jitters of uncertainty run down my legs. I wonder if Al has brought the boys like I asked him to. I've missed them these past days.

When we're invited to turn around, I pivot and open my eyes. The first smiles I see are from Brennan and Trevor. They both rush in and throw their arms around me. I bend down, smell their Johnson & Johnson-scented heads, and squeeze them tight. Both in shorts, collared shirts, and sandals, the boys look like they've grown taller in just five days.

As I straighten up, I notice Al beside my mother. She smiles. He doesn't. I step toward them, and reach out first to hug Al. As I get closer, I notice a cold breeze between us. His face is blank. No smile, no smirk, no nothing. I search his dark eyes, looking for clues and choose to send love with mine. He keeps his hands stuffed in his pockets while I hug him; it's like I'm embracing stone. I hug him tight anyway. I turn to my mother, finding comfort when she says, "Hi, sweetie," and reaches out to hug me.

"Hi, Mom! Thanks for taking care of the boys and for being here with them. It means so much to me." I look around. "Is Dad here too?"

She tries to let me down lightly by whispering, but I am annoyed at the concentration it takes me to hear her. "Uh, this was a little much for him last time, I think. Out of his comfort zone. He sends his love." Her words burn a bit. I think about the coincidence that both my father and my husband are unable to move out of their own way to make room for me in this important moment. But instead of dwelling on them, I return back to the present.

I explain to all four of them that I'll be speaking for a little bit about my experience and lead them to find seats beside me in the large circle of chairs.

The leadership team welcomes everyone. As I look around at the full hall, I'm surprised by how many people are here. Families and friends of all the participants, plus graduates of the program who've come to celebrate the new additions to the community.

When I hear Madonna's "Like a Virgin" blare through the speakers, I know it's my cue to make my way up front. Familiar with and connected to the essence of Madonna because of a significant exercise earlier, I dance into the center of the room and move to the music as if no one is watching. My group-mates are shouting, "We love you, Madonna!" and I smile at the claps, cheers, and whistles I hear. When the music fades, I walk to the podium, my heart beating fast, and reach into my pocket for my notes.

"I'm Michele, and I am a triumphant woman!"

"Yes, you are!" responds the room.

I clear my throat and begin. "I thought this was going to be a seminar about leadership at work, but it's been so much more than that. I've spent eight days in this room finding out who I am. I've recovered some lost parts of myself and reconnected with a little girl inside who wants to play more and find the simple joys in life again. I've learned to identify feelings and communicate with others more effectively. I understand better how and why I behave the way I do in certain situations. I'm walking away today with some great strategies to deal with conflict. I'm taking my huge heart out into the world along with love and forgiveness. I've found it for myself as well as for others."

Before returning to my chair, I introduce my husband, children, and mother, and then recognize and give thanks to my group-mates, the facilitators, and all the coaches. I'm already anticipating the transition back into the real world after spending five full days cocooned in support.

After all participants share, the whole room is invited to stand up, hold hands, and listen and sing along to the words from "The Greatest Love of All," written by George Benson, and sung by Whitney Houston. The last part makes me teary: "And if by chance that special place, that you've been dreaming of, leads you to a lonely place, find your strength in *love*."

For the drive home, the boys are eager to ride with me in my car. They both sit in the back of my Lexus, and I keep looking at them through my rearview mirror, feeling gratitude for being their mother. I think for a moment how I must take good care of myself in order to take good care of them. I play the song gifted to me by coaches at the close of the training, "I Ain't Movin" by

Desiree, savoring all the lessons about learning to love myself and speak up for myself. I tell the boys a little about what I learned at the training, that I've missed them the past week, and that I want to hear about the fun they had with Grandma and Grandpa. Brennan and Trevor both start talking at once, and begin bickering back and forth. When their voices escalate in conflict, I speak with confidence and compassion.

"Hey, boys! Hey. When I hear you talk like that and I see you slapping each other in anger, I feel frustrated and sad. I'm guessing you both have lots to tell me about your weekend, so how bout we take turns sharing, okay?"

"Wow," says Brennan, "that training must've been good, Mom. You're really listening now."

CHAPTER 23

AUGUST 2001

In the days since the training, I keep thinking about all the love, beauty, and honesty that came to life in that drab hall. I have a new sense of inner peace and calmness I didn't know could exist. I'm excited to bring this to the school year, where there has been a major update: the school district has agreed to let me share the principal role with another administrator as co-principals. This means I'll be working part time in order to spend more time with Brennan and Trevor—something I never would've felt was acceptable to do before the training. I know now that I am worthy enough to ask for what I need.

Al walks through the door from the garage after work. He still hasn't asked me one question about the training. I've recognized a frustration within me that he never shows interest in the things that are important to me. Regardless, I walk across the travertine floors and greet him with open arms. He hugs me back. We chat about local traffic and the new restaurant opening up nearby. I talk to him about how Trevor's adapting to his new preschool. Suddenly, Al changes the subject.

"You've gone from crab to happy clam lately," he states with a tight-lipped smile and a sprinkle of sarcasm.

"Really? You think so? Like since I've done the training?" I ask with too much enthusiasm, hoping he's finally acknowledging what I've been wanting him to notice. I'm bursting to share more as I pull new dishes from the cupboards.

"No, Michele, *not* the training. I mean since we moved, since you've had this beautiful house to live in, since I gave you the chance to work part time, since you've had no commute," he replies with clear annoyance, wrinkled lines forming above his brow.

"Yes, Al, all of those factors along with what I got out of the training have added up to my happy clam-ness."

Al's eyes narrow and stare straight into mine, dagger-like. He just stares, saying nothing. I feel an icy cold front. It scares me. So I decide to voice that too, following as best I can the tools from the compassionate communication model I learned at the training.

"Al, when you stare into my eyes like you are right now, I feel fear. I imagine that you are very angry and that you don't like what I just said to you."

I'm proud of myself for being clear and honest, but when I see his eyes widen in response, my shoulders tense. I prepare myself for his reaction.

"How dare you put salt in my wound?"

"What? I don't understand."

"You know I didn't support this training, and I am the victim here—not you. Now you're totally selfish and concerned only about you. Unbelievable!"

He turns to stomp away, like a three-year-old having a tantrum.

Victim? How is he a victim? My thoughts swirl around his every word and scathing stare, yet I choose not to be defensive. Instead, I try a more gentle, yet confident approach.

"It was not my intention to put salt in your wound," I announce calmly as he walks away toward the seven-foot water fountain just installed in the entry hall. "I don't understand why you are so angry that I did this training. Can we talk a bit more about it?"

He turns around and steps quickly back toward me. He has the look of a caged animal.

"You abandoned me that weekend. It was the first night here in our new house, and you chose to be totally fucking selfish. Now you have come back even more selfish. That training? It ruined the relationship we had before, and it's all your fault." He shoves me hard in the shoulder, which is not typical of him, and adds, "Don't you bring up that training *ever* again!"

I freeze. My courage to speak up is halted by hostility. Tears well up fast in my eyes.

He points at me, his voice emphatic. "I haven't done anything to deserve this," he says. "God, I can't believe how I am being made out to be the bad guy after all I've done for you."

He shakes his head, turns away, walks over to the couch, sits down, and turns on the TV.

My heart beats rapidly through my rib cage. I'm shaking, but remain frozen in the same spot. I know I don't deserve to be treated this way. I also know that for hours, maybe even days, I will again be punished with the silent treatment—just like when I was a child and my father was angry. I can't just suck that up anymore. It's too painful. The thought that replays over and over in my mind is: *How can this training, which was so good for* me, *be so bad for* us? *And what will this mean?*

I drop the boys off at my parent's house for a couple of hours as I head to the first night of six weekly meetings for graduates of the summer NLI training. The minute I step into the conference room of the office building, I feel the container of safety and kindness. Hugs and smiles fill the room, and although several participants attend by conference call, all ten of us are present along with a handful of staff. When my turn to share arises, I don't hide my vulnerability.

"I'm angry and hurt that Al isn't interested in what I've learned about myself, and how important this personal growth experience has been for me. He thinks I'm totally selfish, and it's been an icy return ever since I got home."

"If one person in a relationship changes, the other is forced to change too. It's like a teeter-totter effect," Kate, one of the lead facilitators says, picking up a drinking straw to demonstrate. "When one person does things differently, the other has to adapt too, and it's a balancing act."

I nod in understanding, and some of my group-mates add comments also. Most suggest I stay in the present moment in the centered place I've found and not allow Al to send me into a tailspin.

"I think Al is a taker, not a giver. I saw the blank look on his face at the celebration. I think he might feel uncomfortable and not see himself on the same plane as everyone else in the room. Underneath, he might be scared," offers Brad with a shrug of his shoulders.

"Yeah," says Isaac. "I think he's afraid he might lose you, Michele. The reverse side of that is that he actually loves you very much. He just isn't showing it."

"Well," adds David, "I think Al acted like a real dick at the celebration. You're way up here, Michele," he adds, motioning a high bar above his head. "You stay there. Don't let him pull you down."

Nancy and Christina add their perspective to the mix. I feel support and encouragement to endure, and rely on tools from the training.

Staff members encourage me to stay strong, but loving, and remind me that I hold the power and strength to face these challenges. I nod. I know I am worthy. I know I am stronger than I think I am. I know I am glad I took the training even if Al is not.

CHAPTER 24

SEPTEMBER 2001

I wake up with shakes to my shoulder and the sound of Al's voice. I immediately think one of the boys must be calling for me.

"Is it Brennan or Trevor?" I say sleepily and watch his mouth to read his lips. He raises the handset of our home phone.

"No. The phone, it's for you." I look over on my nightstand to see the time. It's 5:52 a.m. I put my hearing aids in fast and take the phone in my hand.

"Hello?"

"Michele, oh my God." Michele Miller, the co-principal that works with me sounds frazzled and desperate. "Turn on your TV."

"What?" I don't think I've heard her correctly.

"Just turn on your TV. Quick. Just watch and listen for a bit and then call me back."

She hangs up fast. I never turn on the television first thing in the morning, but I do what she says and switch on the screen in our bedroom. The image of the World Trade Center in New York City with a hole through one of the towers and smoke filling the sky emerges. Katie Couric and Matt Lauer state confusion about what has happened beyond the report that it appears an airplane has hit the tower. They speak of unanswered questions and speculations that it may have been intentional rather than accidental.

While cameras still show both Twin Towers in Lower Manhattan, Katie Couric speaks more about what they are learning about the crash. A second airplane comes into view on the screen during the broadcast. It directly hits the second tower, and a sonic boom of explosion follows. Chaos and horror ensue.

"Oh my God!" I place a hand over my mouth and stare, then grab the handset and dial Michele Miller's number back. As we each hold an ear to each other while looking at multiple images of people running in fear and hear reports of people jumping from the burning towers, reports of a terrorist attack on the United States are confirmed. Michele breaks the silence.

"Some teachers have called me to say they're too upset to teach today. They might stop by and drop off some lesson plans."

"No. We're all going to be there today. Together. For the kids. Let's get dressed and get there okay? I'll see you at 7:00."

I rush to get ready and am grateful Al can take the boys to school.

On my drive, I think about Christina. She lives in New York City at the Broome Street dormitory where she is a resident advisor and a student at NYU. I dial her number and listen to unanswered rings. I leave her a voicemail telling her I hope she is all right and to please call me when she can. I tell her I miss her and love her.

By midmorning, the United States is declared to be in a national state of emergency. Both Towers of 110 levels collapse, and the

Pentagon burns. There's word that another plane has crashed in Pennsylvania. Reporters confirm that four different commercial airplanes had been hijacked as part of a planned terrorist attack on America. More information surfaces that as Americans mourn, Palestinians celebrate.

Teachers look to me all morning for leadership and guidance. They express concern about having no training about how to talk with children about something like this. At recess, we meet in the staff room to strategize.

"Michele, what do we say? How do we explain this? How do we answer their questions about why someone would deliberately fly a plane into a building to kill others along with themselves?"

"Look, I don't know the perfect answer to that either. But my gut instinct says we need to be loving, strong, compassionate, and united. We must accept their feelings and questions, and let them know that sometimes, us adults don't understand either. There is no way to make sense out of something like this. We just do the best we can."

Another teacher asks if I can write a script for them to use to make a statement to the students. I agree to compose something and disperse it as quick as possible.

A parent approaches me outside the front office. She's shaking her head in disbelief, and I notice she's crying. When she moves closer toward me, I give her a hug. Through sobs, she tells me that she knows someone who was in a hotel next door to the World Trade Center during the blasts. She escaped in her nightgown into a street of chaos and confusion. I hold her while she cries more.

Another parent comes to speak with me. She's holding her daughter's hand.

"I didn't know if I wanted her to come to school today. Can you guarantee me my daughter will be safe here? That there will be no acts of terrorism?"

"Uh, I can't guarantee, but I promise you we will do everything we can to keep her safe here."

After this hectic day, I am eager to pick up and squeeze Brennan and Trevor, make dinner for all of us, and sit together around our dining table in our home to celebrate being together safe and sound.

My cell phone rings while I'm placing dinner dishes on the granite countertops in the kitchen. I pick it up and see it is Christina calling. Her voice is full of congestion.

"I saw the smoke out of my dorm window this morning. Tons of smoke, and then I saw the second tower get hit. That first tower, it was a symbol of strength, wealth, and prominence. It crumbled into nothingness." I hear her cry.

"Oh my God, Christina. I can't imagine how scary it must've been to witness that."

"After the second tower fell, we prepared to evacuate the dorm. We walked with the masses in attempt to escape Lower Manhattan."

She adds more detail of eerie silences and overwhelming uncertainties. She tells me she's okay, but I hear her pain. I wish I could reach through the phone and be there for her.

"The skyline will never be the same, Michele, and I don't think I will be either."

The following days feel long and full of varying emotions as additional details emerge. September 11 will forever be remembered as the largest death toll on American soil from a hostile, foreign terrorist organization. What touches me most through all this sadness and grief is the random acts of kindness expressed from sheer strangers, and the sense of unity and solidarity that's emerged. The American flag flies on cars, hilltops, banners, and sweatshirts. It makes me think of what I'm grateful for. What's important to me in life and what's not.

CHAPTER 25

NOVEMBER 2001

Since it's getting close to winter, and I love the feel of warmth, I push the button on the wall to create an instant gas fire in our bedroom fireplace and let the flames invite me into relaxation mode. I plop down on my bed with a cup of chamomile tea after tucking in Brennan and Trevor. This is the time of day I enjoy most after long days of work. I create a kind of peaceful ritual before bedtime lately. I light a lavender scented candle on my nightstand, push play on my Bose to hear ocean music in the background, and eagerly open my top nightstand drawer to find the cover of my journal. I pause for a moment and consider how healthy and authentic it feels to be the journal writer I am again. I've completed three in the past several months.

I think back on the first journal I ever had. It was right after Paula Edwards, the popular girl in the fifth grade, exiled me from my group of friends. In between my sniffles and sobs after trying to run from the school, Mrs. Bowen told me that writing could help me feel better. Her suggestion was to start a "journal" and write about my feelings.

"You can write poems or anything you want," she said as she compassionately placed a composition book full of blank lined pages in my hand.

I slowly reached up and took it from her, thanking her politely while still working hard to extinguish my tears. I wasn't convinced I would ever use it. But that day, I went home and began to write in it. I wrote a poem first. A poem by my hurt ten-year-old, friendless self. I still remember it to this day:

> I don't have many friends today,
> but maybe soon another day.
> As I walk with my head up high,
> looking in the big blue sky,
> I think of times when I'm alone,
> like when I eat an ice cream cone.
> When I go to bed at night,
> I think about the next day's light.
> When the morning comes that day,
> I think about the price I'll pay.
> But I know I am a good person,
> and nobody else is like me.

After that, journal writing became a hobby, a refuge, and a lifeline. A sacred place where I can authentically express myself—my true feelings, wishes, hopes, fears, and dreams.

Taking a sip of tea, I realize I've lost touch with this outlet over the past years. When I write, I don't record where I've been, what I've done, who I saw, and how it went. Instead, just as Mrs.

Bowen suggested, I write about how I feel. Writing in my journal gives me a break from logic, sense, judgment, and just plain old over-thinking. I don't worry about correct grammar, spelling, or even making clear sense. I can choose to be sarcastic, childish, or bratty, or I can be vulnerable, explorative, wise, and philosophical. Regardless, I pour myself out onto the page, watching my pen race across the terrain like a well-trained marathon runner. I am surprised at my ability to write candidly even when emotions are senselessly swirling around inside the blender of my head. As a result, embedded within the pages of my journals resides the person I truly am.

After writing for a while, I get the urge to go back and read what I've written in prior journals. I've never done that before. Usually, I complete an edition, add it to my collection on my top closet shelf, and leave it there to collect dust.

The first journal I remove from the shelf is the one I finished three months ago, just before I started the training. I flip through with my thumb and forefinger, hearing the pages fall together softly before stopping to a random page in the middle. My eyes scan the marks of ink and land on some sentences where I speak about my relationship with Al. Certain words call out for my attention: *Powerless. Afraid to speak up. Disconnected. Hurt.* I sigh a breath of discontent and turn away. I stare into the fire in the fireplace. My vision softens and my thoughts dance over those words.

I think back to earlier this week.

"Hey, Brennan and Trevor, no eating in the living room. You need to come back and sit at the bar or the table."

They look from me to Al who is sitting on the couch, new bag of nacho cheese Doritos in his lap, chomping away.

I know what is coming next.

"How come Dad gets to eat in here and we don't?" Brennan asks.

"Aw c'mon, boys. It's okay. You can eat in here too!" Al says automatically, gesturing to them to come sit beside him and continue watching *The Simpsons*.

I can't believe what I am hearing. We have talked about this.

"Hey, Al, I thought we want to keep the new carpet clean and enforce the practice of not eating in the living room," I add casually as if it's just a friendly reminder, hoping he'll remember and make a quick correction.

"Nah, it's fine," he barks back while looking straight ahead at the television, crunching chip after chip.

Feeling unsupported and dismissed, I stand there like the lion without courage in *The Wizard of Oz*. And as much as I will it to be different, I know I won't have the courage to broach the topic again later. This pattern is already ingrained too deeply. None of our prior disagreements have been readdressed or resolved. We just toss them into a mountain of disregard.

Now the pages in front of me describe this sensation over and over—the thick layer of fog that rolls between Al and me. It's made of the same smoggy haze of defensiveness, assumptions, judgment, and fear. Cold, damp, and dreary, it seems to blanket sunshiny moments and make them completely disappear.

I speed up the pace of my page turning. It's as if the journal has fallen into the hands of an eagerly assigned private investigator searching for more clues, more evidence. I feel surprised and disturbed to see it all so clearly written, staring back at me in my own handwriting. Some of it I don't even recall writing.

I grab the journal prior to that one, the journal before that, and even scour one way back from 1998, looking at the contents of my heart sprawled out before me. I see right here that he's told me a number of times, "I know you better than you know yourself, Michele." But of course, I know that this is not true. So why don't I challenge him? Why do I stay silent?

Inside me, a battle begins to brew. One side of me, the side that has gathered all the evidence, pushes to use these findings as proof that I better start speaking up. The other part wants to hear none of it. This side believes that if I keep my true feelings stashed away in the confines of my private journal and not in the consciousness of my daily life, attracting conflict, I can avoid the issues, focus on the positive instead, and just be happy.

Before I put the first drops of ink into my new journal, I take a deep, cleansing breath, and hear the question inside my head I know it's time to answer in the real world: *Are you going to keep writing the same stuff and keep your mouth shut? Or are you going to stand up, be brave, and let Al see and hear what you really feel?*

CHAPTER 26

DECEMBER 2001

After bedtime stories and tuck ins are complete, I'm lying in bed on my back, holding the book *Living in the Light* by Shatki Gawain, which was recommended following the NLI training. I feel as if Gawain is speaking directly to me as I read a chapter about the importance of listening to your intuition. She explains that intuition is a knowingness that resides in each of us, and that by learning to listen to it, we can connect to an inner wisdom and allow that to become a guiding force. She believes that most of our personal and social problems occur as a result of being driven by fear, suppressing our emotions, and not following our intuition.

I reflect on the affirmation I wrote for myself on index cards, which I taped up where I see them daily—in my car, on my bathroom mirror, by my nightstand: *I am a secure worthy woman, and I trust my own instincts.* I am starting to more clearly understand what it means to listen to the whispers of this intuitive voice and how to follow its guidance.

I flip to chapter 18, which is titled Health, and begin to read. The hairs on my arms prick up as I take in the black and white words jumping off the page. "The body can show us what is and isn't working about our way of thinking, expressing, and living."

She goes on to list a variety of health conditions, but I let out a little gasp when I see "Hearing Problems: Needing to shut out external voices and influences; needing to listen more to your inner voice. *I don't have to listen to anyone else. I listen to, and trust, my own inner voice.*"

This takes me right back to the question Brett asked me months earlier that replays often in my mind: "What is it you perhaps don't want to hear?"

I kick off my covers, open the second drawer in my nightstand, and grab *Heal Your Body* by Louise Hay to reread what she's written about deafness. Sure enough, on the chart of ailments toward the end of the book are the words: "What don't you want to hear?"

Is this just a coincidence—these two authors teaching me the same, exact thing? One of the quotes I've highlighted in Gawain's book catches my attention from where it lays open on my comforter: "There are no coincidences." I have to laugh.

I slip back underneath the silk sheets to finish chapter 18. A suggested meditation on health is next. I focus on several rounds of inhale and exhale. Then I close my eyes and silently ask myself the suggested questions: "What do I need to heal for myself now?" "What does my body need?" Shatki Gawain suggests being open to intuitive feelings that arise right away but also for answers that may arrive days later.

The last sentence I read before I put the book down is, "Know that you can heal yourself and that limitless wisdom lies within you."

I switch off my bedside light and turn on my side for sleep. I feel a bubbling of hope. A stirring promise of possibility. I am listening. I am hearing the message. I am willing to believe.

Several nights later, I walk into our master bathroom and glance over at the tub. Surrounded by rich, warm, shiny marble, it sits grandly on two steps, as if on a pedestal. It exudes sanctuary and refuge, but for some reason, I haven't used it much. I walk over and turn on the warm water, hearing the calming cascade permeate the quiet. I decide to keep my hearing aids in and not submerge my head so I can avoid the loneliness of silence.

Below the sink in the cupboard, I find a packet of bath beads. After I pour them in, I'm disappointed to watch them quickly dissolve in the clear silky water, so I reach for the pink bottle of Mr. Bubble and add two streams. While the water fills, I walk down the hallway past our wedding portrait on the wall and Al sitting in the living room, watching television with his feet up on the black leather couch. In the kitchen, I grab a wine stem and pour a glass of Napa Valley Chardonnay. He doesn't turn to notice me, nor does he speak any words. With the boys fast asleep, the only voices I hear are characters in the current episode of *Mind of the Married Man* and Al's intermittent laughter.

I return to my little oasis and place five white tea-light candles in a row before I step into the warm water. Taking it slow to submerge myself and stretch out, I admire the abundance of bubbles and move them in closer, as if seeking to protect the vulnerability beneath the surface. Lately, I've become preoccupied with looking for some kind of compass to navigate the uncharted waters Al and I seem lost in. I have had opportunities to bring up the topic, yet it never seems like the right moment. Time and time again, I've chickened out and thought, *No, not now. Maybe next time.*

I'm settling into relaxation mode, surrendering my head to the inflated pillow suctioned to the porcelain, when Al walks in our bedroom and glances over at me. No smile, no scowl. He's wearing a green sweatshirt and sweatpants, and sheepskin slippers cover his feet. I scan his eyes for some kind of window to glimpse through, but they looked glazed. I flash a friendly smile anyway and raise my glass toward him.

"Hi there!" I initiate.

"Hey. Just sitting in there, relaxing?"

"Yeah, it's really nice. Want to join me?" I sit up a little straighter.

"Naw, I don't take baths." There's a hint of irritation in his tone. He stands still, focusing on me.

I feel the awkwardness in the air between us. A quote flashes up on my radar screen: *"There is no time like the present."*

"Al, will you come sit beside me here for a minute?" I motion for him to sit on the edge, extending my hand toward his. He looks cautious more than curious. A moment later, he steps toward me. He places his hand in mine, but my excitement fades when I realize I'm clasping a lack of interest. With queasiness in my stomach, I look deeply into his dark blank eyes and see what looks like curtains drawn. I push through my fear.

"Al, I'm really afraid for us—for our relationship, our marriage. Umm, I think we could do a better job of communicating. And I, uh, recently got the name and number of a reputable counselor in the area. I'd really like for us to go see her together. You know, to work on us. Help us be happier."

My foot moves nervously underneath the bubbles, and I know

I sound too much like a Dr. Phil's Script of the Month. I'm tapping to the rhythm of worry, awaiting his response.

"Why don't you go by yourself?" he matter-of-factly inquires.

I remain calm. I am prepared for some resistance.

"Because I want us to be a team. I want us to tackle our issues together. I think if we communicated better, Al, we'd be a better *us*."

He releases my hand without hesitation and stands straight up. Looking directly down at me like a lawyer in court moving in for the cross-examination, his eyes are seething.

"No, Michele, you're the one who likes all the touchy-feely stuff—the workshops, the self-help books, the psycho-babble—not me. Why don't *you* go to counseling? You're the one with a problem, *not me*. You go and let me know what she has to say."

He turns toward the door to leave, but stops and pivots back reluctantly in response to my last desperate plea. "Wait. Please, Al, I'm begging you. This is so important to me. From the bottom of my heart. Please. Will you please just try it—just go even once with me?"

"No!" he shouts, and marches out of the room.

I bring my hands to my face, my foamy knees to my chest, and I cry and cry in this bathtub for what seems like hours. Sounds emanate from within that I don't recognize. I wonder if I let myself cry long and hard enough, if the tears will make the water overflow onto the limestone floor.

But after sitting with myself, salt residue staining my cheeks, something different starts to emerge. I think about all the hard work I did to learn more about myself in July and how much benefit came from talking candidly about my feelings to coaches. *Okay,* I say aloud to the Universe with some strength, *then I will go by myself.*

CHAPTER 27

2014

Relaxing in the ship's front lounge, I am reading my book quietly, a Stella Artois on the table. One of National Geographic's 2013 Adventurers of the Year, Mike Libecki, had given a presentation a couple nights earlier about the mountain climbing expeditions he's done all over the world. I was impressed with his courageousness, and when he walks past me, I decide to tell him. He thanks me and takes a seat to continue our conversation. I share that I am feeling separate and different from all the brave, adventurous people on the ship like him.

"Do you ever feel fear?" I toss out the question I've been curious about since day one.

He smiles and responds with a quiet, compassionate tone.

"We all have our vulnerabilities, our fears. I'd be concerned about someone who claims to feel no apprehension or fear."

"Hmm, I guess to me, it seems like it's not much of a factor for you."

He looks perplexed.

"For you to do all the expeditions you do, in all the unknown conditions and circumstances, I wish I was less afraid, more adventurous and brave than I am."

"Ah, I remember you. That first morning...I think you were in our Zodiac. You shared that you were overwhelmed by the scenery. You weren't ready to touch the land."

I nod, feeling self-conscious and embarrassed to admit this.

"For you to speak that truth is vital. It is way more brave and courageous of you to know and listen to your gut instinct, trust, and go with it. So many others would just lie and say, 'Oh yeah, no problem. I'm good to go.' It took more guts to stay in that boat with your truth than it would've to go along with the group. Good for you."

"Really?"

"Yes. If I was going on an expedition and I had the choice of taking someone like you, or someone who says they aren't afraid of anything, I would take you. It's all about making informed, calculated decisions. It has nothing to do with not being afraid."

The light-filled room after midnight isn't what's keeping me awake tonight—it's scenes of the trip replaying through my mind. I see how I am in fact much more brave and courageous than I think I am. I made the assumption that being brave is about being fearless. I was wrong. Fearlessness is not about not feeling fear. It's about meeting fear face-to-face, eye-to-eye. Standing in the center of the ring with it, shaky legs and all, feeling its force and impact, and pushing through it anyway—whether that means staying in the boat or stepping onto a new land.

The next morning, during the brief Zodiac boat ride across Admiralte Bay to King George Island, the right leg of my waterproof pants leans into Gordon's left while we ride with eight others. Chilly whips of wind in my face cause me to drop my chin closer to my chest and pull up my neck gaiter to cover my lips. The inflatable boat's engine holds a consistent hum until we approach the shore of a still-functioning Polish scientific research station. Even though it's not sunny, I wear my sport sunglasses to soften the brightness of white all around us. Gordon invites me to exit ahead of him, and I scoot my bottom forward along the rubber edge, swing my legs over, and step with waterproof boots into waters full of black rocks covered in snow and ice. I listen to the crunch of each step I take. It sounds as if I am stepping on piles of potato chips. When I reach the shoreline, I notice bones—bigger than dinosaur bones—lying across the beach. I turn around and look at Gordon, who seems to have already read my mind. "Whale bones. I think they're relics of the past whaling culture." I grimace at envisioning these gentle, majestic giants being stripped of their flesh. Even skull bones are strewn about this beach as we walk and explore.

The colony of Adélie penguins we approach makes no effort to avoid us. These black and white beings are medium-sized like the Gentoo penguins we've seen, but their necks are shorter and their bills thicker. A white ring surrounds each eyeball, but otherwise, they are pure black and white. The only color evident is the pinkish hue of their webbed feet. I kneel down on one knee, keen to savor this moment with them. I know this is our final Antarctic land experience before we make our journey back to South America.

I concentrate on the sound of their little squabbles and wonder what they're saying. They waddle and strut their wings out behind them like airplane wings. Several seem just as curious about me, as I am about them, as they approach, displaying white bellies in clean tuxedos. I wonder if they can feel my joy as I remove my sunglasses, take a more solid seat on the snow, and just stop and stare into their dark eyes for several quiet minutes. I sense they want me to realize that I have an indomitable spirit, that I too can experience the toughest of challenges and still come out victorious. Penguins demonstrate adaptability in harsh conditions. They are walking contradictions in that they're birds, yet aquatic and flightless. They're resilient, social, and particularly expressive with sound. I don't think it's an accident that I've come here to Antarctica and had an opportunity to experience these unique creatures. I stand up and take several photographs, feeling grateful for my new, wise friends.

Gordon and I venture into the open office of the Polish research station. One section inside is a post office. Once a month, an airplane lands here from Chile and picks up mail for the mainlands. It costs extra to purchase a special stamp to signify letters or postcards have been physically mailed from Antarctica. We sit in warmth, accept the cup of tea offered by friendly staff eager to have visitors, and I write postcards to my parents, both my sons, and my best friend, Laura, while Gordon pens them to his parents, daughter, and son. We buy the fancy stamps for all of them and, even though it's mid-November, hope the recipients receive them before next year.

Gordon's ungloved hand reaches for my covered one, and we walk along the shore of black rocky sand as clear surf washes up close by. We stop to watch a group of penguins jostle and bump into each other at water's edge, making loud *"gak"* noises, as if deciding who will be the first to dive in. Once one goes in, several others follow, some sliding on their bellies and slipping down thick rocks to enter. They zip effortlessly into the dark, cold wet.

"Do you know what the official name is for a group of swimming penguins?" A researcher from the station calls out as he wanders by. We turn and see him standing, wearing a Ushanka, a fur cap with long earflaps.

"Uh, a flock?" Gordon asks.

"No. They are a 'raft' of penguins when they're in the ocean."

"I would never have guessed that!" Gordon replies with a chuckle. Then we turn back around and watch this raft of penguins swim with ease together out into icy unknown.

CHAPTER 28

JANUARY 2002

It's the day of my first appointment with Janet Bailey, the counselor. It only took me five days to get an appointment after gathering up the courage to call her. I'm nervous, but ready.

In the waiting room, I sit on a love seat, eyeing the books on the shelves and inspirational quotes on the wall. Soothing instrumental music plays softly. I wonder where I'm even going to start when the door holding the sign "In session" opens. Two women emerge from the room, and I am unsure which one is Janet until I hear the other say thank you and step toward the door.

"You must be Michele," Janet extends her hand as our eyes meet. Her smile is bright beneath auburn shoulder-length hair, and she wears a simple dress over her plump body. I am caught off guard by the unexpected sadness that suddenly washes over me. I open my mouth and stammer, "He…he was supposed to be here with me—my husband. I wanted so badly for both of us to come here together." I let out public sobs, unusual for me.

"Well, you can't make someone do something they don't want to do. You can't control him. But what you can do is work on you. And that's where we will start, okay?"

I nod and follow her into the room. For the hour that follows, I notice how freeing it feels to express with vulnerability and truth about everything I'm holding inside. I share with her about my health issues and hearing impairment, the recent self-awareness I've learned after attending the training, my struggles communicating with Al, and doubts about the strength of my marriage.

Janet is intuitive, observant, and validating. She offers that my second and third chakras are blocked around feminine power and expression, noticing that I'm struggling with one-on-one communication and intimacy. I've never heard of chakras, but I'm open to her assessments. She continues, asking reflective questions.

"What attracted you to Al in the first place?

"Um, I didn't like him at first. He had long hair, a cocky attitude, and a sign in his dorm room above his bed saying 'Speed Limit 69.' But I was attracted to a glimmer of a sensitive side he didn't show others but would reveal to me sometimes. I admired his strength, humor, and uncomplicatedness. He seemed even keeled, unemotional, and not high maintenance in any way."

Janet listens, nods, and jots down a few notes before responding.

"Has anyone ever described you in those same terms?"

Her question surprises me. I've never thought about it before. But while I repeat the words in my mind, I consider the image I have presented to the world that I've "got it all together."

"Hmm, maybe. I guess so."

"I'm wondering if you were attracted to those qualities in him because you saw a lot of yourself in the reflection. A lost self of you, seen in him."

"Maybe. The lost self I feel as though I'm recently beginning to find."

"Yes. Tell me more about that, Michele."

"I saw confidence in him and someone who was funny and carefree and not afraid to be goofy, and certainly wasn't worried about what others think of him. He had the bad boy image, free and uninhibited. I think I've learned lately that I locked up the little girl within that wanted to be all those things. I thought that by letting her be that way, she would be too much trouble. And if I wasn't good enough, I might lose my mom."

I squirm in my seat a few times because it feels warm in the room. Janet uncrosses her legs and reaches over to open the door a bit, letting me know no one is in the waiting room.

We go on to discuss ways I can work on improving my relationship with Al. She stresses that I can only change me, and be responsible for myself. That I'm not responsible for Al. That I have no control over anything he does, says, or feels.

"Many of your words and actions stem from a need to seek approval. You need to express rather than impress, okay? Do you see?"

"Yes. I do. I'm working on that. Sometimes I do it well, and other times I don't." I nod and look at some crystals she has on a table.

"It's only by being authentic—truly being true to who you are—that you can make the choice to continue with this marriage. It is a choice, you know."

Her comment lingers. I make another appointment to return in two weeks.

Music plays through speakers of the portable sound system in our upstairs home gym. I turn up the volume before beginning my run on the treadmill and set my timer for fifteen minutes, up from the ten minutes I ran at the beginning of my exercise routine five months ago.

Outside the window, looking over a hillside at the rear of our house, I see rainy winter skies put on a show as my running shoes start their rhythm. I'm happy I'm working part-time and get to have mornings like this. After taking the boys to school and returning home, I meditate for five or ten minutes and then work out.

When I glance out the window next, I am surprised to see snowflakes falling from the sky. Not icy specks, but large beautiful snowflakes with detail. I've never seen snowfall in this part of Northern California. I get off the treadmill, jog downstairs and out onto the wrap-around porch. The street is quiet. The air smells clean and crisp. Snowflakes fall with a quiet grace and confidence. A sacred stillness lingers. I breathe and watch the white of my exhale merge with the cotton balls and flakes, and feel consumed by joy.

Snowflakes settle on the grass, the porch railing, and individual leaves of plants and trees. I stand there and savor each second. I open my mouth and taste the soft, fluffy wetness.

As if an unexpected gift has been placed on my doorstep, I am so grateful I can be here to witness it. Hairs stand up on my arms but not from the cold temperature. From awe. I think about the phrase "be present in the moment." I've heard it and read it in books but until now, not clearly understood its meaning. And I realize in this moment what it means. I feel part of nature. One with it. And it's because I'm experiencing what it's like to be right here, right now.

CHAPTER 29

FEBRUARY 2002

I let the water of the shower stream down the back of my hair and head for a few moments. Not having to rush to work this morning, I bask in the invigoration of my two-mile run. I stand there, eyes closed, breathing rate back to normal, and just feel.

"Mommy?"

I open my eyes but don't see him.

"Trevor, I'm in the shower, sweetie. Be out in a sec."

"Is it a stay-at-home day today?" His four-year-old voice full of hope.

Oh shit! Just before I respond, I suddenly step out of the spray and reach up with both hands to my ears, reaching to remove the right one first. *How did I forget to take them out?* My heart sinks at the thought that I've just shorted out four thousand dollars of technology I rely on daily. But my eyes widen as I realize they aren't in!

I shut the water off. Grab a towel and wrap it around me.

"Trevor, are you still there?"

"Yeah, I'm here on your bed waiting. C'mon." His words sound pure and beautiful, and fill my whole being. I'm stunned. I hear every word.

I dry myself fast and move to the middle of the master bathroom. I pause to look in the mirror, almost to make sure it really is me in the reflection. My smile widens as I grab the jeans I wore yesterday and a sweatshirt from the top shelf.

As I approach Trevor and bend down to his level, he speaks again.

"I said, is it a stay-at-home day today?" his words are so clear.

"Oh, sweetie! I heard you! And it *is* a stay-at-home day today!" Two tears fall from my chin.

"Why are you crying, Mommy?"

"Because you have the sweetest voice I've ever heard, Trevor!"

I wrap my arms around him and pull him in close. I realize in this moment that I'm hearing Trevor's voice with my own ears for the first time. Ever. He was eight months old when I lost my ability to hear. After a lengthy embrace, I look at him again.

"Trevor, I can hear you without having my hearing aids in." He gives me a puzzled look, and I understand he has no idea what that means. But I do. I think it means my hearing is getting better.

We walk out of my room and down the hall together. Al has taken Brennan to school on his way to work, so it's just the two of us at home. No preschool for Trevor on my day off. A "stay-at-home day." When I pass by the front door, I open it wide and just stand there. Listening. Bird songs and chirps. A car passing by. I know it's not just my imagination. Even the closing of the door after a few minutes sounds different to me. Clearer.

As I make pancakes for Trevor, I keep asking him questions

so I can continue listening to his sweetness for as long as possible. When I return to my bedroom to dry my hair, I glance at the box sitting on the counter containing my hearing aids. I'm reluctant to put them back in just yet. Instead, I turn the hair dryer on high, launching through the regular routine, taking in the new sound of Conair. I put on makeup after that, listening carefully to the sounds of my fingers rummaging through contents of my drawer. *Can this really be?*

After grinning at myself in the mirror, I put my hearing aids in now like I've done every day for almost four years and head back to the kitchen where Trevor sits at the counter, finishing a glass of orange juice. I pick up the phone and call Dr. Wong's office. The nurse asks what message I want to leave for him.

"Could you please tell him that I think I am hearing better? This morning, I heard voices and things that I haven't been able to hear in years, without my hearing aids."

She assures me she will.

I tell myself not to watch the clock, but at 11:25, when it does, I jump toward it with a drawn-out, enthusiastic "Hel-lo?"

"Hi, Michele. You sound like you're expecting a call." My mom's English accent is on the other end.

"Oh hi, Mom!" I try to not sound let down, and then remember I have call waiting, so I can chat for a bit.

"Everything okay?" she asks.

I wonder whether I should tell her. I want to shout out this news to the world, yet I don't want to get ahead of myself. Secondly, my mom's more available and attentive when I'm sick or hurt than during times when I'm elated or celebratory.

"Mom, I think I am hearing better today! I actually thought you might be the doctor's office calling me back because I left Dr. Wong a message. I really think I am hearing things today without my hearing aids. Like Trevor's voice when I was in the shower. Mom, I actually thought I had my hearing aids in because I heard him so clearly. His voice. It sounds so beautiful. And I even opened the door and heard the birds outside too."

"Really? Oh, sweetie," she responds. "That's wonderful."

I don't want to get her hopes up or mine for that matter in case something happens and I don't hear again tomorrow, but I hold a strong feeling for the first time again in years. Faith.

Later the same day, the phone rings. It's the nurse from head and neck surgery at Kaiser. I've got a scheduled appointment with Dr. Wong in two days.

1985

I'm nineteen and standing in a room of complete white. My mother sits on the edge of the white bed, facing two dark-haired men wearing white lab coats. It's cold in here, and it smells like Pine-Sol. One doctor is asking my mom questions while the other watches and takes notes in a manila folder. My mom's jet-black curls stand out against the stark surroundings. She sits, holding tightly clasped hands in her lap. Her knees looked glued together. Her back is rounded as if she's trying to diminish her tall slender frame. She looks timid, unconfident, lost. And I guess she is. Why else would her doctor call me while my dad is out of town on a business trip and insist that I bring her here immediately? Sutter Memorial Hospital. Seventh floor—Psychiatry.

"Are you feeling suicidal today, Marie?"

"Yes," she whispers back, her chin falling to her chest.

"Do you have a plan?"

"Yes," said in the same monotone voice.

"Have you ever attempted to take your life before?"

The silence lingers. After raising her gaze and looking directly at each of the doctors, she slowly turns her head around to look at me. I think I see shame and sorrow interspersed in her lifeless blue eyes. She doesn't know that her answer won't shock or surprise me. In fact, I'm curious about whether or not she will tell the truth. I wait. She scratches her head, shifts in her seat, and her eyes dart from the doctors to me and back to them. It feels as though a layer of fog is quickly rolling in.

It's me who cuts through the awkward silence.

"I know, Mom. Okay. I know. You can answer the question." My voice sounds confident and compassionate. Like I could be on the team of doctors around her.

Her dark, well-groomed eyebrows raise.

"You? You do? But how?" Her eyes trying to recall a memory about being truthful with me about herself, her past, her story, yet knowing she never has.

I don't feel like going into it now. Don't want to relive being the sixteen-year-old sitting at the dining room table beside my father holding a glass of scotch after I'd finally asked the burning question I'd been holding inside for years: "What the hell is wrong with her? Why does she have to go 'lie down' all the time, and why can't she make simple decisions like what to have for dinner? Why isn't she normal and like other mothers?"

She looks me directly in the eyes. "Did Dad tell you?"

I let her out of her discomfort quickly but say gently, "Yes, he did," while sending love back to her eyes, and wondering at the same time if I will get in trouble for breaking the promise of secrecy.

My mom begins to cry and turns back around to the doctors. "Yes," she nods. "I have."

They ask to see her purse, and when she lifts it up from her side, one of the doctors unzips it and dumps it upside down, spilling all the contents out onto the bed. He sifts through her things and removes the mirror, the nail file, the prescription medications, even the pens.

"For your safety, we will need to hold these while you are here."

Seconds later, the doctors tell me it is time for me to leave. I nod and step toward my mother, swallowing against the large lump in my throat. I lean down and wrap my arms around her thin and bony shoulders. "I love you, Mom."

"She'll be okay," one of them assures me as I turn toward the door.

Yes, but I am not sure I will be. I want to say it, but don't.

I leave the sterile room and walk through blank hallways. The walls are harsh and cold. I want to run, but I feel as though I can't breathe. I rush through the double glass doors to outside color.

What I don't know at this time is that her stay won't just be a few days. She'll remain in the ward of white for weeks.

CHAPTER 30

FEBRUARY 2002

I'm fidgety while I sit and wait in Dr. Wong's familiar small office, with nothing pleasing to look at on the walls, nor any magazines to flip through. How can this kind of environment be healthy to work in day after day? When the door creaks open and he enters in his lab coat, I am eager to blurt out my news.

"I think my hearing is coming back. I'm hearing things without my hearing aids."

It's the first time I've held a smile in this room. It remains until he speaks.

"I know you want to hear better, Michele. Could it be wishful thinking?"

It's as if the scoop of ice cream sitting on my sugar cone has just rolled off onto the ground.

"No, this is real. I know for sure that I am hearing things that I otherwise haven't been able to without my aids."

I consider taking my hearing aids out right then and there to show him, but his voice is one of those low tones. I'm afraid my experiment might backfire. It's still new and raw, this improvement.

"There may be a slight fluctuation in the inflammation level of your inner ear, allowing you to hear a bit more. Probably temporary. I don't want you to get your hopes up."

His words and matter-of-fact-ness are not the response I expect.

"But, can we do another hearing test and see if my levels have improved?"

"Let's schedule another appointment in two weeks and see where we are then."

He offers a gracious smile, pushes himself back on his rolling stool, and stands up.

It's been sixteen days. I'm counting. I know my hearing is coming back. I'm sure of it. I'm soaking up every sense of sound. I've been woken up by Brennan in the middle of the night. I've been listening to music and watching television programs all without hearing aids. The pureness of sound is what stands out to me. I can't get enough of it. I keep doing visualizations of my ears filling with light and clarity. I'm learning to listen to my own intuition, I'm talking with Nancy and Christina on the phone often, and I'm writing in my journal every night, focusing on what I am grateful for.

Al is happy for me that my hearing is better too. I'm telling him what it's like to hear again, especially Brennan and Trevor's precious voices, while we're in our bathroom getting ready for work one day. I think I see his eyes well up at my descriptions. That's rare.

"You've never heard Trevor talking to you before without hearing aids in, right?" He buttons his white Club Room dress shirt and adjusts the collar.

"That's right. He was eight months old when I lost my hearing. Brennan was three, so I didn't hear his voice for that long either. I can't even explain how happy I am about this. How much it means to me to hear them so clearly." I pick up my comb and move it through the tangles of my wet hair.

When Dr. Wong enters for our follow-up appointment, I watch him walk to the sink and wash his hands.

"I have great news to tell you!" I blurt out before he has finished drying them.

"Okay, what's that?" He asks as he turns to face me. I hear his voice before being able to watch his lips.

"I am hearing even better. It's coming back," I announce.

He grabs his scope.

"All right, let's take a look. Go ahead and take out your hearing aids."

"I don't have them in." I speak slowly, watching his expression of surprise unfold. I beam.

"What?" he says. "You haven't been wearing them?" He wants to smile too, I can tell.

"I do still at work, but I know I am hearing better, doctor. I am hearing when I am in the shower, my sons' voices are clearer, and

I'm even catching some whispers. I'm hearing you right now, and it's been just over two weeks now. It's not fluctuating. I think it's gotten even better."

"Okay, that's great. But I don't want you to have high expectations and then be disappointed later. You have had a severe hearing loss for four years. Four years. The reality is that after that much time, it is highly unlikely that it will improve and stabilize long term."

He looks at me with compassionate eyes.

"Well, when can we schedule another hearing test? I know it will show I am improving," I ask optimistically.

He glances down at the chart in his hand and shares that my regular six-month audiological exam is scheduled for April 2, five weeks from now. I take a deep breath and sigh on the exhale. I even hear my own breath better.

"Wait here for a second." He moves to the door, opens it, and walks out, leaving it ajar. I listen to the stark white walls in this small examination room, thinking of how often I've sat here, straining to hear his low-tone voice. The usual hum I hear is definitely fainter too. I know I am not imagining all this.

Doctor Wong returns to the room with his eyebrows raised.

"Analissa is going to squeeze you in. Can you do the hearing test now?" he flashes a smile of kindness.

"Oh yes! That would be great!" I stand up with nods of eagerness. It's the first time I am excited to return to the soundproof vault for testing.

Analissa recognizes me. We talk briefly about what improvements I notice. She guides me to the room and chair, the same one I've sat in so many times. But as the meat-locker type door shuts this time, I feel less intimidated. I place the headphones on, and we proceed through the same progression of audiological tests, beginning with beeps. I raise my finger when I hear a sound, whether it is low or high in tone. Next, she adds in white noise, and I raise my finger when I hear a beep no matter how loud or faint it sounds. Then comes the one that has always been the most challenging for me: repeating back the given word. While I am sure I have missed some, I am hearing and discriminating words better than the last test back in November.

Analissa swings open the heavy door and stands looking at me with big bright eyes.

"You are right! You are hearing much better. There is significant improvement, Michele. Come, let me show you the comparison."

I feel exhilarated, vindicated, and strong. Tears of happiness arrive when she shows me the charted pages of my test today compared with the last. With a couple of frequencies nearing the normal range, there is no doubt about significant improvement in many areas.

"I knew it!" I exclaim. "I am *so* happy!"

"I don't know if it will continue to improve, but I am hopeful," Analissa says, holding up her fingers crossed, smiling at me. I notice emerging tears in her eyes too. We hug.

Sitting again in front of Dr. Wong right after these hearing tests, he looks at me and then shakes his head in disbelief at the written results.

"I can't tell you why you're hearing has improved. I can't give you an explanation. It's very rare."

"It's okay. I don't need an explanation." My voice is clear and confident, and I'm speaking with respect and truth. It doesn't matter what medical reasoning he has or doesn't have this time. I know there's more to this than what the practice of medicine can explain.

Later, I sit propped up in bed, candle light glimmering on my nightstand, instrumental music playing softly in the background. I take out my journal and write.

I honestly believe and know that my improved hearing is the result of listening better to myself—listening to my feelings, acknowledging them, being with them, and not judging them. I feel so much more in tune with who I am and what I feel, need, and want. I think I'm starting to see the results of listening to my inner voice and trusting that guidance. I'm feeling a stronger connection with the Universe—like I'm being given the opportunity to learn an important lesson here. I want to keep learning and growing and developing a strong spiritual connection. I want to keep being present in every moment and enjoy moving with the flow of life instead of resisting it. I'm so thankful for these weeks. I want to be grateful every day for the sense of sound, and never ever take it for granted.

CHAPTER 31

MARCH 2002

"We're going skiing on Thursday and Friday. It's spring break, and you don't have to go to work," Al announces from the couch as I place the last dinner dish in the dishwasher.

A familiar tightness constricts my throat, warning me to avoid conflict and alter my plans, but my hesitation is noticeably brief this time. During weekly conversations with Nancy, she reminds me that I shouldn't allow myself to be a doormat. That I have the right to speak up. I want to engage differently with Al.

"Umm, Al, I'd really like to be asked if I'd like to go skiing. It helps me feel as though I have a choice. Besides, Anne asked me if we could get together Thursday before she has her baby, so I'd have to consider that too."

"We are going skiing on Thursday. There's no reason we can't."

Did he not hear me? I try again.

"When you make plans for us without asking me, I feel angry and resentful, and I imagine that I have no say about what I would like to do or not do. I'd really appreciate it if you would ask me, Al."

I am proud of myself for being honest, utilizing the suggestions from Janet, my counselor, to be brave, speak slowly, kindly, and not use too many words.

"I can't believe this," his voice rises. "You are so self-absorbed and selfish." He slams his magazine on the table and looks at me, fire emanating from his dark eyes. "This is *bullshit*."

Because I consciously did not draw my swords, I am stunned by the sudden blow.

"But—" I respond with desperation, attempting to escape the escalation before he cuts me off right as I emphasized the "t."

"No," he interrupts. "You know what? I'm gonna just do things with my boys and forget about you."

He stands up and stomps out of the room, mocking me as he walks down the hallway to his office with a high-pitched tone, "I need a choice. Well, boo fucking hoo," adding a fake sobbing noise to the mixture before slamming his door. The family photo falls off the wall and crashes to the floor.

I feel anger rise from within my stomach into my throat as if a volcano is erupting. Unpredicted lava spews from my mouth, "You're an asshole!"

I stand motionless, feeling alone and confused, staring at the empty hallway. I let out a sigh, wondering what I could've done differently. What I can own. Certainly, the asshole comment is not the type of communication Janet would advocate. I wonder for a few moments how people in other marriages do it. How they argue, how they disagree, how they speak up, and how they resolve conflict.

I know what will follow for me. No responses to my questions, no return of eye contact when we pass by each other. No "good night" or "good morning" reciprocated. Silence. Just like the cold quiet room I've been left alone to stand in.

Later, I wonder what to do in my punished aloneness. I consider writing in my journal until the idea of writing a letter to Al emerges. After all, it's one of my most effective modes of communication. I think perhaps I can better state what I wasn't able to successfully communicate verbally, and I feel a flash of hope at the possible outcome.

Careful to use "I" messages and not point fingers, I craft my words on white binder paper with my favorite black pen. Phrases flow across the page such as, "My intention tonight was to share what's true for me. I do want to spend time with you, Al. It's just that I'd like to be asked if I'd like to go skiing. It would help me feel involved in the decision and as though I have a choice." I write more about my feelings along with my desires to connect and have a loving relationship. At the close of the letter, I apologize for my angry outburst. When I put the cap on the pen and hear the click, I feel satisfied. Hope mingles with sadness. I put the letter in an envelope and, knowing he probably won't be coming to bed anytime soon, leave it where he will see it in the morning.

I glance over at the unopened envelope before leaving the quiet house for work. I envision Al reacting well to my heartfelt words. I anticipate him talking to me again later, and mending our quarrel.

I return home after a productive, positive day of work in a cheery mood and walk into my bedroom, kick off my heels, change my clothes, and then I see it. Face up, the pages of my letter lay there with bright blue highlighter marks all over it. Confused, I picked them up and scan. Al has boldly highlighted every one of my printed "I," "me," and "my." At the top, in all capital letters with the same blue marker, he's written, "IT'S ALL ABOUT YOU, ISN'T IT? YOU ARE TOTALLY SELFISH!!!!!"

I feel my legs shake and give way. I slide my back down the wall of the bathroom to the cold stone floor. I raise my knees to my chest and let my head fall into my hands. It's like I've fallen out of a three-story window, and I'm struggling to breathe. My chest cavity squeezes in a vice. Tears rush from my eyes, and I listen to the cries emerging from deep within that I don't recognize as my own. How can I be so terribly misunderstood by the one person in the world I want so badly to know and love me for who I am? I am dizzy with despair, and a void permeates the room. The distance between my husband and me feels infinitely wider now, when this letter was meant to bring us closer.

We do not speak of it again, this letter. I choose to leave it alone after hearing his words in my mind say, "You're looking for problems, Michele." It has become Al's standard reply almost every time I initiate a discussion about us, our communication, our marriage. But he's wrong. I'm looking for solutions, wanting badly for him to join me in the quest for closeness and connection. I've been to five counseling sessions on my own now. I'm craving deep, meaningful conversations full of interest and love. Longing for gentle touch and affection. Some indication that we'll get through these turbulent times.

I've been hiring a babysitter occasionally to pick up the boys and make them dinner so that I can join a girls' nights out or attend weekly support-group meetings for training graduates. Instead of having to rely on Al in order to make plans or disrupt his routines, I'm enjoying this arrangement and the freedom to do more things to benefit balance in my life. Al goes away a few times a year on guy trips for fraternity alumni weekends and out-of-town mountain biking events. I figure I deserve the same.

Since the fall, in the aftermath of September 11, I've been thinking about visiting New York City. Christina still attends NYU, and Nancy wants to go too. We've been discussing plans for a girl's weekend together.

It's the first time that instead of asking Al for permission, I make arrangements and share them with him after, just as he does with me. While he's in his office typing an email, I ask him if I can come in for a moment and coordinate calendars.

"I'm looking for flights to New York City to go visit Christina for a few days. Nancy wants to fly there from LA and go too."

"Oh, when?" I hear his fingers stop typing on the keyboard.

"Two weeks from tomorrow. I'll have Thursday and Friday off work and return on Sunday. Mellani is all set to get the boys to and from school, make them dinner, and help out over the weekend too if necessary." I have my planner in hand with a pen. It feels business like, but effective.

"Okay. Flights probably aren't that expensive these days to JFK," he says.

I purchase the non-refundable tickets several minutes later, and as I come back into an empty kitchen, I do a little happy dance.

The morning of my flight, I have a line of seats to myself. Rows in front and behind me are completely open. It seems eerily unusual, but I rather like the feeling of being on some kind of huge private jet. After the safety announcements, I think about how the future is unknown. None of the passengers on the planes on September 11th had any inkling of a reason to not travel that day, and none of their loved ones had any reason to worry.

I arrive at JFK airport feeling free and adventurous, and jump in a cab to get to the dorm on Broome Street near NYU. While I feel light and joyous, the reflection in the rearview mirror of the cab driver's dark face reveals noticeable sadness. I initiate conversation, and it isn't long before he shares his heart. I don't struggle to comprehend his words and accented voice. I'm surprised. I listen to him talk with my ears, my "real ears" as I've begun to call them. My hearing aids are tucked safely in my purse, just in case.

"This place is so different now. My childhood friend from India, my best friend who I immigrated with, worked in Tower 1 on Floor 104 and was killed on September 11th. After that, I lost my job, and my hope."

My heart feels heavy for his burden, and I know I can't imagine the pain he's holding. He shares more. I learn that he has been driving a cab now for two months and that his hope is gradually beginning to return, coming from the kindness and compassion from his passengers.

"The terrorists can't win if we don't give up, so we must continue to stand tall," he preaches. He speaks of his newfound respect for former mayor, Rudolph Giuliani, and how the new mayor has big shoes to fill. He comments on the severe decline in tourism but predicts that within the year, it will change, much like he has.

I consider my own changes over these past months as well: the joy of knowing myself better and feeling happier within, getting my hearing back, yet going through so much turmoil in my relationship with Al. I wonder if like this driver's prediction, it can shift, adjust, and grow with time. I wonder if he and I are both healing, albeit in different ways.

When I arrive at Christina's address, I pay the driver with a generous tip and give him a hug. I stand on the sidewalk with my suitcase and just listen. An orchestra of car horns, cross walk chimes, high heels, sirens, and conversation. It all feels so new again. I want to take it all in. New York City, the perfect location for celebrating the recent return of noise.

I hug Christina in the lobby of her apartment, her ringlets of long, thick brown twenty-two-year-old hair cascading down her back. Our phone conversations have been meaningful and frequent, but no comparison to face-to-face connection. We decide to just hang out on this first evening after a long travel day. We order take-out Chinese and walk back to her place to watch the movie *French Connection*, and then we catch up on the details of past months until the wee hours of the morning.

I stay with Christina in her dorm room and wake to an open window of clear blue skies and a vast view of tall buildings, and the hustle and bustle on sidewalks below. I stand still, close my eyes, and listen with intention to subway sounds, traffic congestion, and airplanes flying overhead. Christina joins me at the window. She points in the direction where she witnessed smoke-filled skies that fateful morning and relays the horror of her experience. She speaks of our conversation on the phone that day and shows me the route of her evacuation. We discuss visiting Ground Zero to pay respects. We decide to go on Sunday when Nancy arrives.

We walk the streets of downtown, pick up a true New York bagel with cream cheese, and people watch. I feel my chest tighten when we pass by the firehouses with memorials and remembrances outside. Photographs capture the still raw emotions, and flags are prominently displayed. Christina speaks of an outpouring of generosity and kindness within the whole city, and how the resilience of the human spirit has been palpable.

When Nancy arrives, we act like three schoolgirls happy to be reunited outside the training environment. During the daytime, we shop, dine out, laugh, share, and cry. I think about how real our conversations are, and the veils that are lifted when we can be so transparent. We see the Lion King on Broadway, learn subway routes, walk down Fifth Avenue, and bar hop in the evening.

On Sunday morning, after waking up together in Christina's dorm room, we make our way to Ground Zero. We pass one firehouse with a fiberglass Statue of Liberty in front of it. Its creator is unknown, and it looks as if it is guarding and protecting the fire station, which is peppered with photographs and remembrances of the many who lost their lives on 9/11. We pass another station where fifteen firefighters lost their lives. A shrine of gifts and tributes are on display.

When we arrive at Ground Zero, we first visit the museum of photographs surrounding the site along a long chain-link fence. I am taken aback by the handwritten cards, drawings, banners, photos, notes of sorrow, missing person signs, rosary beads, quilts, flowers, and stuffed animals. Thousands and thousands of them line the way to the platform that's been built thirteen feet above the ground of the site. With each step, I reflect on my own personal devastations and explosions these past four years, and even way back into childhood. The seemingly bottomless pain. Looking around today at all the love, empathy, and hope, the overwhelming sense I carry is that of gratitude. For all of it has led me to right here. And I am alive.

The three of us walk hand in hand up the plain plywood walkway that leads to a large rectangular stage with a full 180-degree view of the devastation. We stand in silence and say our prayers for those who lost their lives here as well as the friends and family left behind. Surrounding the huge hole in the ground, clean-up crews still work nearby. Windows of neighboring buildings are still broken, and walls are blackened. While no words are spoken, much is communicated as we all look into each other's glistening red eyes and pay respect.

CHAPTER 32

2014

I t's 1:00 a.m. in our stateroom and the darkest I've seen it. Gordon and I are in our twin beds. My eyes have suddenly opened because all the contents on the small desk have crashed to the floor. It's as if someone opened the door and cleared everything off with an angry swipe of their arm. The chair tips over, the toilet seat cover slams shut, toothbrushes dive off the bathroom counter, cupboards fly open and bang against the wall. I try to stand up to crawl in next to Gordon, only to be pushed back by a ghost hand. The ship is rocking back and forth violently. Yes. This is the Drake Passage.

I knew our Drake Lake entrance to Antarctica was too good to be true. Now we get Drake Shake. No, I am not afraid this time. Instead, I am frustrated. As soon as I get through one big challenge, another seems to greet me around the corner.

On our way to breakfast, Gordon and I walk single file down

the narrow hallway, holding onto the wood-capped railing on the right side when the shoves feel especially violent. Small individual white barf bags have been placed along the rails. Gordon says he isn't feeling very well, and many faces look paler today. Most adventurers are in their staterooms with seasickness. Fortunately, my Scopolamine patch is working well.

We stop and listen to the captain's announcement over the intercom. "This is a serious situation. We are traveling through a hurricane with thirty- to forty-foot swells and one-hundred-mile-per-hour winds. All passengers must remain indoors for the next twenty-four hours."

Sharp booms with a violent rock of the ship cause me to tighten up all the muscles in my body. Like I'm bracing myself. The ship continues to rock heavily. At times, while walking back to our stateroom, I am pushed into walls or have to grab onto something secure, hold tight, and wait. Glasses have broken, chairs lay on their sides, and the sight out the windows is either high black seas or dark gray clouds.

Gordon and I decide the best place to stay through this storm is together in bed in our stateroom. He wraps me in the comfort of loving arms and tells me we will be okay as the water rises and falls over and over outside our window. The repetitive sound of heavy hits of the hull onto angry churning seas worries me, but I know there isn't anything we can do to change or avoid the situation. I allow myself to surrender into the safety and love I feel with Gordon by my side.

It's many hours later when we catch sight of land for the first time again, in calm waters. I feel a sense of peaceful relief. Gordon and I push the heavy ship door open and stand on the deck, holding hands, free of thick gloves for the first time outdoors in weeks. Under blue skies, cars, houses, lush green trees, and purple blooms of Jacaranda paint the canvas of life again. We've arrived at the South American continent.

My first steps on land bring strange sensations between my feet and solid ground. I still feel as though I'm rocking, unable to reconnect with true earth at first. I notice vibrant hues of color as if seeing them for the first time after so many days of white. The sound of engines on the road, car horns, squeaky breaks, and crosswalk traffic signals overwhelm me but make me giggle at the same time. Civilization!

I think back on our voyage and about what is required to stay strong and feel safe and secure in challenging conditions. I realize much comes from within. What I tell myself, what my perspective is, and how mind chatter can help or hinder. I feel close to Gordon, and grateful for his acceptance and love for whether I act out of confidence or react out of fear. I feel as though he's interested in seeing all parts of me. The top of the iceberg as well as those complex depths below. But it's me accepting myself for who I am that's the main lesson. I somehow feel that if I can face uncomfortable conditions—whether a small conflict or trekking up an icy mountain in Antarctica—with a stable centeredness inside me, I can go through anything and come out stronger on the other side.

CHAPTER 33

MAY 2003

My hearing and my health are thriving. I wish I could say the same about my marriage. I don't understand why a happier, healthier "me" seems to be such a detriment to the "us" Al and I have become as a couple.

Our thirteenth anniversary is four days away. As I peruse the calendar on the wall in the kitchen area, and see it falls on a weekday, I suggest to Al that we both take a day off work and escape into reconnection. He tells me he likes that idea, and we plan to take the boys to school that day, drive a couple hours to Marin County for lunch overlooking the Bay, and then head on to Stinson Beach. We agree we can do all that and still make it back by 6:00 p.m. to pick up Brennan and Trevor from daycare. When I visualize us walking along the sandy shoreline, I see our fingers interlaced and our footsteps in sync.

During the car ride on the morning of our anniversary, I share with Al what I'm most looking forward to today—a long stroll together on the beach. I tell him I want us to walk barefoot hand in hand, listening to the ocean waves. He nods and acknowledges my request. Listening to music for ninety miles, we encounter little traffic and arrive early in Tiburon.

We select Sam's as our restaurant of choice. I'm excited by the bright sunshine over outdoor tables and a vast view of the sailboat-filled bay. I remove my sweater to soak up welcoming warmth on my shoulders and arms as we're seated at a table for two. I order a glass of chardonnay while Al orders an Italian draft beer. We relax and settle into mid-week vacation mode, ordering appetizers first. As we watch sailboats enter and exit the marina, I initiate a conversation to reminisce about the time we sailed with Al's parents from Sausalito to Pier 39 and experienced a small fire on board. "Remember the (*sniff sniff sniff*) and the 'what's that smell,' with no idea it was our burning boat?"

"Yeah, that was scary and funny at the same time," Al responds. We both giggle.

I wonder what to talk about next. An awkward silence ensues. While it would be easy to fill time communicating about the kids, I want today to be more about the two of us. I ask some questions about work, comment on some recent updates from friends, and allow some silent moments, hopeful that our ocean visit will more naturally guide us to connection. As we pay our tab and head to the parking lot, I mention to Al again how much I'm looking forward to a beach walk with him.

The moment we pull into Stinson Beach parking lot and find a space steps from the sand, my stomach bubbles with excitement. I hop out, grab the blanket from the trunk and tuck it under my left arm, then take my sandals off and hold them in my left hand. On purpose, I've left my right hand free. I'm hoping that even though

Al's never been much of a hand-holding guy, in public places especially, he will place his in mine today. We walk side by side past reeds and weeds growing on the upper dunes. I tell myself I shouldn't expect him to be a mind reader, and I consider just grabbing his hand right next to mine instead. But I don't.

As miles of sandy beach appear in view, I stop for a moment and greet the sea with a wide smile, as if she's a treasured friend. I listen to the surging wash of surf and waves while we walk toward the water. The smell of seaweed permeates the air, and a gentle breeze brushes my long locks toward the back of my shoulders. We spread our blanket down on the shimmering golden sand and sit side by side. I take a deep cleansing breath and scan the surroundings. Families picnicking, dogs fetching sticks, couples basking in the sun, and seagulls soaring overhead. I watch Al lean back and lie down, Maui Jims still covering his dark-brown eyes. I notice his mountain biking defined calves as he stretches his legs and clasps his hands over his tee shirt. I assume he must be relaxing into the experience of being in this beautiful setting, although in a different way. I listen to child laughter, seagull caws, and waves crashing, closing my eyes on occasion with gratitude for pure sound.

It's less than ten minutes later. I toss out the question like a Frisbee, "Ready for our walk?

No reply.

"Hey, honey?" I decide he must be playing with me, purposely pretending to be asleep, and his twisted sense of humor irritates me. He knows how important it is to me for us to take a walk on the beach together.

I repeat my question. "Hey, Al?"

Again, nothing. He is out. Fast asleep, dead to the world. I consider just making the most of it. Cherishing the opportunity to just sit here on the beach beside him, but I know in my heart, it isn't enough. Twenty long minutes pass. The only change to the scenery is the sound of a shallow snore.

I shuffle, sigh noisily, shift side to side—all in a sly effort to wake him from his nap. He doesn't budge. The more fidgety I become, the less patience I have to remain stuck here. I inch myself forward, set my toes in the sand, and look to the open ocean. For what seems like hours, I contemplate, wonder, and question with angst. Until I realize the reality and simplicity of my decision. I can stay here, or I can walk.

Scooting forward onto the balls of my feet, I stand up. Reluctant at first, I take a cautious step forward then another and another. I look back to find out if he's noticed. My hopefulness is again, not enough. He hasn't budged.

I continue to walk, wanting with all of my being for him to wake up, glance down the beach, and excitedly run to catch up with me, grab my hand, and rescue me from this lonely feeling. After taking twenty more steps, I look back again. Nothing has changed. I tell myself to count at least fifty steps before I stop and turn around again. At fifty-one, I look another time. The realization of *he's not coming* releases the first stream of tears from the faucet. Continuing to walk with blurry vision underneath my sunglasses, and an endless runny nose, I pass through the seaside towns of Resistance, Loneliness, and Fear. When my breath suddenly becomes shallow, I realize there is a strange familiarity to the discomfort and deep pain I'm feeling. I travel back in time to exactly thirteen years ago today. In my mind, it replays like a vivid and colorful movie scene.

We're standing as bride and groom on the porch of what now is officially our first home as husband and wife. Al's tuxedo-shirt collar is unbuttoned. His black bow tie hangs off to one side, resembling him as he sways, trying to place the key into the lock. He pushes the door wide open. I joyfully anticipate the sensation of being swept off my feet in my flowing white gown and carried like a princess across the threshold. Instead, Al stumbles four loud, heavy steps forward and falls on the living room couch. I stare from the doorway. His eyes are already closed.

"Al?"

No response.

"Hey, honey?"

Nothing.

He is passed out. Cold.

I lift my long flowing dress up with both hands to cross the threshold on my own, close the door behind me, and listen to the sole sound of heels on the hardwood floors as I make my way to our bedroom. Soon after entering, I raise both hands over my head and down to the base of my neck to start undoing the gazillion buttons that go down the back of my wedding dress. We have one hour to get changed and ready before our ride arrives to take us to the airport. As I unbutton the first four and notice a struggle to continue, I lift and lower my head. But as I do so, I catch a glimpse of this gorgeous bride in the Cherrywood mirror five feet away. I stop. It's as if she's calling me toward her. Scanning the reflection from head to toe, I feel beautiful in my dress. Silk, beaded, white, flowing, and Cinderella-like, I had tried it on and immediately knew it was "the one." I stand there for several moments, studying every bead and stitch carefully, not wanting to take it off, not wanting the dream to disappear. Not wanting to never wear this again. But then, I actually wonder if I will be able to get this off on my own in an hour. All these buttons. *It wasn't supposed to happen this way.*

I catch my eyes in the reflection. Yet they don't look like mine. Not in this dress. They look like they belong to a frightened little girl, too nervous to speak. I move toward her. Her eyes draw me in closer, begging for trust. We hold our gaze deeply. She whispers to me. I watch her lips move through each syllable, "I made a mistake. I made a *big* mistake," and her eyes close while she looks down. Panic rises in me as I study her. My voice pipes up in the chaos.

"No no no. You're probably just emotional from the day. Overwhelmed, tired, maybe even affected yourself from the champagne." I shake my head, unaccepting of her despair.

"No, wait. I really made a mistake. I want to call my mom. I want to tell her I made a mistake. I don't want to be married to Al." Her words are stronger. She looks deeply troubled.

"What? Call Mom? Oh, no no. We can't do that. What are we gonna say, Michele? 'Uh, thanks for the fabulous wedding that was beautiful and that everyone loved attending, but I don't want this'? No! We cannot do that. We married him. We committed. We took and said the vows. It's done. We will make it work."

"But I . . ."

"No more. Go on your honeymoon. You are married now. You already said *I do.*"

The eyes reflecting back are full of confusion, deep despair, grief, and regret. I don't know what to do except back away from her image and pretend that this little "incident" never happened. In order to do so, I make another vow in that moment. To never tell anyone about this. And I've kept that agreement. Until now.

Waves rush in and lap at my feet, bringing me back to the present moment. The amplified sound of *I made a mistake* lingers in my ears. I wonder if it's time to finally listen to that inner voice I've discounted time and time again. But what about my precious boys?

Will I ruin their lives if I leave Al? I continue to walk and walk, focusing now on nothing more than each present step. I know I'll need to turn around eventually.

When I do, I notice a seagull soaring gracefully overhead in front of me. She flies solo but exudes confidence, peace, and freedom. I think about what I teach Brennan and Trevor by pretending my marriage is fulfilling and happy when it isn't. What could I model to them by gaining wings of my own? I then catch the eye of a passing stranger walking alone also. His compassionate gaze and tender smile moves through me as if to convey an important message. A voice deep within says, "Through the darkness, there is light."

I begin to review the parallels of the anniversary afternoon to what my marriage has become. I've been in the waiting place. Waiting for things to be different. Waiting for circumstances to change. Waiting for him to join me. Waiting for him to wake up and participate in our marriage instead of sleeping obliviously through it. *How long am I going to wait? How unhappy will I allow myself to become?*

When the blanket comes back into view and I see Al still asleep in the exact same position, I realize this is the day to finally make the long-drawn-out, gut-wrenching decision I've been reluctant to make. "I'm going to walk on my own," I say aloud to myself while taking the remaining steps. "And I'm going to be fine."

CHAPTER 34

2015

The start of my day begins in silence. Every day does now, but it's this kind of silence. Intentional. Chosen. Each morning, as the light of a new day emerges, regardless if we are home or traveling, I rise and meditate.

On this particular morning, just before sunrise, I sit cross-legged on a blanket, moving my hips gently side to side to nestle both of my sit bones into the soft grains of sand beneath me. I aim for a straight posture, aligning my spine and feeling the connection between my body and the earth. I settle into myself with comfort, knowing I'll stay for a period of thirty minutes. Pacific Ocean waves roll in fifty feet in front of me and fill my ears with their rhythmic ebb and flow. While daylight is present, the sun isn't visible yet behind me. A soft, cool breeze brushes my cheeks. My arms rest gently on each thigh, palms facing upward. When I take a quick look at my surroundings, I notice I am alone on this long stretch of beach except for two seagulls soaring overhead. I have my Insight Timer app on my iPhone set for a thirty-minute session, and press start. Two basu bell chimes fill the empty air.

I greet this space with a few deep breaths before I allow my eyelids, on a deeper exhale, to close. I concentrate on my breath, focusing my attention on the sensation of air entering my nostrils and expanding my stomach, torso, and lungs. I pause for a moment at the top of my breath, and then gradually release air back through my nostrils. I remind myself that I have nowhere else to go right now, and nowhere else to be, but here, with myself. I notice a thought creep in that says, *Oh shoot. I forgot to buy butter yesterday. What am I going to use on our English muffins this morning?* And another arises: *I should make sure I call Mom and Dad back today like I said I would.* I let these and any other thoughts that want to distract me pass as if they are clouds drifting overhead across the sky. I know they can wait. Right now, I am just here breathing in and out. Even when I hear a seagull screech or an unknown sound in the background, I let it be there, strive to not attach to it, and instead, bring myself back to my inhale and exhale. I focus on the breath in, which I think of as life, and then on the exhale, which is a release of what no longer serves me.

While I concentrate on breath, I scan my body for areas of tightness or restriction. *Ah, my neck, my lower back.* I use the next inhales to visualize bringing air to both areas of constriction. Healing air.

I maintain my gaze beneath closed eyelids, not on images that arise as much as evidence of light. Rays, tubes, specks, or sparkles of light sometimes glow in my centered stillness. I've learned with practice and experience to just be with what is, not try to alter the circumstances more to my liking. To just be in silence without fear and discomfort, to connect with it. Embrace it. And stay with myself.

It's not long before I feel a softening. A simple surrender into silent space. I let go of any additional sensations of resistance or constriction. I notice and release any fear that wants to intrude or distract. I recognize tenderness. A calling forth of my originality, my most true essence and authentic self. I've come to learn this space is one of love, trust, faith, and belief.

I open my ears and listen to the call into self rather than into external noise. I uncover and access an infinite well of wisdom and power in solitude. Yes, by just sitting in silence, breathing, and being. Silence.

The bell chimes three times. I take a few moments to bring myself back to the present moment. Wiggle my toes, stretch my fingers, and take two deep breaths. After a third inhale, I release with a verbal chant of "Ohm," which comes out of my mouth sung as, "Ohmmmmm." This is a hymn of the Universe. I chant it just once to remind myself that I'm worth speaking up for. I'm worth listening to.

As I open my eyes, I hear the sounds of life's new day and look around. Sunlight now glistens on ocean water. Three pelicans glide just above the blue, and a jogger runs alongside surf. Someone else tosses a tennis ball and a black Labrador retrieves it. I uncross my legs and turn around to look behind me. Gordon stands on the back deck of the beach house we've rented for ten days, holding a mug of coffee. He waves with his other hand, and I wave back, then he lifts his cup toward me in offer of one. I nod.

I stand to greet Gordon as he walks up beside me and extends the mug.

"Good morning! How was your meditation practice?" I absorb his deep voice, his loving gaze, and the comfort of the arm he puts around me. I tell him I couldn't wait to pick my place in the sand and settle in, but he's nodding before I even finish my sentence. He knows. It's one of the reasons we stay near the beach a couple of times a year. He pulls me in close for a kiss, and then we both stand facing the surf and sip. The waves sound powerful as they move in and spread white foam on the shore. Then as they pull back into the whole, there's a thick silent pause. This reminds me of breathing.

Gordon suggests we go for a walk. We place our cups in the sand beside the blanket, and he takes my hand, interlacing his fingers with mine. As we start our steps along the stretch of golden, I notice how moist sand mixes with surf and cradles the shape of our feet as we walk side by side. I glance over my shoulder and grin at the path of footprints we leave behind us and then squeeze my grip on Gordon because of the wrap of happiness I feel being married to this man wearing Tommy Bahama trunks and no shirt.

I think back in time to when Gordon and I struck up a friendship after coaching a training fourteen years ago. We met for coffee, spilling vulnerable feelings and lending helpful support to one another while we each navigated difficult divorces. In my mind, I can still hear his emphatic words that followed a particularly deep conversation, "I just want to make sure you understand that we are meeting only as friends," and my reply of how relieved I was that he'd clarified that. We were in total agreement. When we met several weeks later again for coffee, he stated the same again, "I said last time that I wanted to make sure you knew we were just friends."

"I know. I know. I got it."

"Well, I've been thinking about you a lot. And I'd like to take you out to dinner sometime." My mouth hung open.

"Oh no," I replied, as I placed my hands over my eyes.

"Oh no? What?"

"Well, I don't want to lose my friend."

"You're not going to lose your friend. It's just dinner"

I explained that my favorite movie of all time is *When Harry Met Sally,* and I didn't want anything to change between us. He'd become one of my best friends.

That image is followed by the memory of the Halloween I was going to spend without my boys in 2003. Brennan and Trevor were scheduled to be with their dad that long weekend, and I had shared with Gordon that I was dreading not being able to get them dressed in costumes and watch them go door to door for the first time.

"Want to go to Chicago for dinner?" Gordon asked on the telephone.

"You mean the new restaurant in Folsom called Chicago Fire?"

"No, I mean Chicago. The city. Mortons."

"Uh…uh…well, I've never been to Chicago."

"Neither have I. Let's go. I'll get plane tickets."

Unbeknownst to me at the time, that spontaneous travel trip to a new place neither of us had ever been, born from the basis of friendship, and Gordon's desire to help me turn a weekend of dread into a weekend of excitement, would be the first of many shared travel adventures. We married two years later in 2005. Gordon is still my best friend.

Gordon tells me he's ready to jump in the ocean. I smile and watch him walk into the surf, brace himself, and surrender to the chilly waters as his whole body plunges into a wave. He glances with a grin toward me to check whether I've seen him, so I wave back to let him know.

While Gordon lingers and floats on his back in the salt water, looking into the cloudless sky, I listen to the sound of waves and childhood shrieks of laughter in the distance and think about how grateful I am that I am still able to hear. Oftentimes, I just stand and listen to nature and the noises of everyday life, absorbing the gift of this important sense. While there are times I still miss a word or sentence, I continue to value pure sound, function well, and am not afraid to ask for a repeat. While I'm no longer a patient of head and neck surgery, neurology, or audiology, I still include a number of healthy practices and regular treatments in my life in order to maintain optimum whole body health—meditation, exercise, yoga, spending ample time in nature, eating healthy foods, journal writing, time shared with girlfriends, counseling, gratitude lists, attending retreats, and scheduling appointments regularly for acupuncture, massage, and cranio-sacral therapy. I still keep handy a copy of Louise Hay's *You Can Heal Your Life* book and reference it often for any ailments that arise, reminding myself of affirmation and being an active participant in my own healing. I am more healthy and happy than I've ever felt.

I glance over my shoulder to the space where I began my morning seated in silence, and am transported back to the last anniversary I shared with Al on the beach, watching him fast asleep on that blanket. I marvel at how far we've all come since then. Just last week, Trevor graduated from high school; and Al and his girlfriend, Julie, Al's mom, brother, sister-in-law, and grandmother as well as I, Gordon, Brennan, both my parents, and my brother and sister-in-law all stood together with Trevor in celebration. We did the same in 2012 for Brennan's high school graduation, and I remember thinking as I looked around our dinner table following the ceremony that Al and I are great co-parents. Al is and always has been a loving father to Brennan and Trevor. Although we finalized a difficult divorce in 2004, in the years that followed, we shared custody fifty-fifty, spoke regularly on the phone, and always both attended and shared birthday parties, important school meetings and parent conferences, graduations, and basketball games. Unlike a lot of the other divorced parents, we always cheered on our children while seated next to each other.

While I picture myself walking alone on the beach that day, desperately looking back at Al asleep on that blanket and making one of the hardest decisions of my life, I wonder if all the voices on the outside had to be muted for four long years so I could listen for the whispers calling me from the inside. Brett's question of "What is it perhaps you don't want to hear?" I found shocking— even offensive and accusatory. But I realize now how right he was. I didn't, at that time, hear love for myself or know how to turn my gaze inward. At that time, I wasn't able to sit in solitude on a blanket and just be there for myself. I was too busy looking externally for all the answers.

I think about something I heard recently: that the letters in the word *listen* are the exact same letters in the word *silent*. This doesn't surprise me, as I know how closely tied those two words truly are. That's why I choose this kind of silence every single day. So I can listen.

As Gordon comes out of the water and back onto sand, he pauses for a moment and looks at what's being washed onto shore. I watch his hand reach down and retrieve something. He holds it out toward me as he approaches and tells me it's a gift. I open my palm, and he sets it gently in my hand. A perfectly round white sand dollar.

"Let's keep walking!" he says while grabbing my other hand and pulling me down the beach.

ACKNOWLEDGMENTS

ith love and gratitude to:

Joanne Fedler, for the depth of energy, support, encouragement, mentoring, guidance, promotion, and opportunity you have personally provided me every step of this incredible writing journey. This book's entrance into the world with you by my side means so much. You and the entire Joanne Fedler Media team have changed the publishing industry with creativity and innovation. Special thanks also to Nailia Minnebaeva for a cover design that takes my breath away and Norie Libradilla for excellent support and final edits.

Laura Lee Mattingly of kn literary, for being a dream editor. You helped me strengthen my final manuscript into a full-length book I am proud of.

Rachel Resnick, for the realness and rawness in your own memoir, *Love Junkie*, and for becoming a mentor and coach to me. You taught me the importance and value of writing vivid, sensory-abundant scenes, and reminded me to celebrate successes along every step of the way. I hope I get to pay it forward like you did, my friend.

Members of my writing sisterhood: Kylie, Lisa, Marcia, Louise, Judy, Xanti, Cheryne, Kerry, Pip, Mylee, Athina, Lorraine, Georgia, Catherine, Donna, Robyn, and Katrina. You've provided such consistent support, encouragement, inspiration, and collaboration.

Brett Miles, for asking me the profound, life-changing question, "What is it you perhaps don't want to hear?" You encouraged me to look inward. It's become habitual now, and it makes all the difference.

Ron Wu of NLI and Chris, Gayle, Debbie, Phil, and Maril of the Authentic Leadership Center and the invaluable eight-day training called Leading from the Center. I can't thank you enough for being an integral part of my own self-awareness and personal journey.

Doug Stoup and Ice Axe Expeditions, for an incredible twelve-day trip to Antarctica that turned out to provide a perfect frame for my story and teach me even more about myself.

Christina Joy, for wise insights which have impacted me more than you know. You've championed me in writing my story since its inception. I still visualize the butcher-paper pieces pasted on the walls of my living room while you helped me tease out themes and create strong character development—always believing that my dream to write this book would become a reality.

My buddy, Nancy, whose friendship, laughter, and love have taught me to never doubt that I am more than good enough. Thanks for being a sister through tough hours of personal-growth work, encouraging me to speak up and to "never be a chicken." Wisdom I hold close still today.

Village Acupuncture, and especially Noriko, Anna, Sarah, and

Catherine. I know one of the reasons I remain so healthy and vibrant today is due to regular acupuncture sessions with you. I am so grateful, not only for your skills, but your beautiful, caring hearts.

Teachers along the path of my journey, whether spiritual, inspirational, and/or literary, who've influenced and helped me these past writing years without even knowing it: Louise Hay, Wayne Dyer, Eckart Tolle, Shatki Gawain, Oprah Winfrey, Deepak Chopra, Davidji, Brene Brown, Marianne Williamson, Neale Donald Walsh, Glennon Doyle Melton, Gabby Bernstein, Elizabeth Gilbert, Cheryl Strayed, Elizabeth Lesser, Craig Hamilton, Jeff Carriera, Alex Myles, and Sarah Blondin.

Laura Duffin, who from the beginning offered to read and give feedback on writing pieces that came to shape the form of my first (shitty) draft, to the reading and re-reading of every revised draft since. You've been there every step of this journey with me. For years, you consistently supported and encouraged me to keep going, keep writing, and helped me tread water whenever I fell into pools of self-doubt. Your belief in me helped me believe in myself. I am forever grateful to you, my BFF.

Mom and Dad, for your unwavering support and pride in me writing this book. Despite my conveyance of deep personal experiences, your belief that my work may inspire others is a tremendous gift, not only to me, but the world. I love the close bond we share, and I wouldn't trade you guys for any other set of parents. Mom, thanks for staying here on the planet despite the darkest of your days, and for loving me as much as you do. You're not only my mother, but also a treasured friend. And Dad, I want you to know you've made a difference in my life, still do, and always will. You and I will always have "Say You, Say Me," and I'll never tire of how proud you are of me.

Brennan and Trevor, for being my precious sons. Being your mother has been and remains my greatest joy. Brennan, even during your earliest years, your wisdom has taught me so much about myself. Trevor, hearing the pure sound of your voice with my ears for the first time sparked new life and hope within me. It's my favorite chapter in this book and still makes me cry (with joy) every time. I love you both up to the moon and back again.

And finally, Gordon Brown, for being my loving, patient, supportive husband, and my biggest fan. You've been unwavering in your belief of my success. Thank you for your patience during endless hours spent writing behind a closed door, and for knowing I needed to honor this agreement with myself even if it took years to accomplish. You teach me what true love is, and what teamwork is about. I love you with all of me, and bet you can't wait for my second book!

About the Author

Michele Susan Brown is a writer, author, and speaker based in Northern California, where she lives with her husband, two dogs, cat, and the wild birds that visit her backyard feeders.

A former elementary school teacher, principal, and district-level administrator for eighteen years, Michele now spends time following her passions: writing, meditation, exercise, time in nature, swimming with wild dolphins in the Bahamas, and traveling on unique adventures all over the world with her husband, Gordon.

Michele enjoys connecting with others and engaging in deep discussions about the importance of listening to our own intuition, being brave and vulnerable, and the freedom found in authenticity and truth.

You can connect with her at www.michelesusanbrown.com, and/or write to her at michelebrownauthor@gmail.com

CPSIA information can be obtained
at www.ICGtesting.com
Printed in the USA
FSHW020414060319